# What Others Are Saying about This Book . . .

"Let me tell you about my hero, Archie Willard. As an occupational therapist, I come from the clinician side. Archie of course, comes from the patient side. Our work has overlapped and intersected in many ways. I have interviewed Archie several times for publications and videos as well as having collaborated on projects. Archie and I continue to be passionate advocates for health literacy."

—**Helen Osborne, M.Ed, President of Health Literacy Consulting, Founder of Health Literacy Month, Producer and Host of Health Literacy Out Loud**

"I met Archie in 1992 when we traveled to Russia and Estonia with a delegation of thirty other zealots—all of us interested in dyslexia and learning how a different culture views learning disabilities. Archie and I connected immediately. I was attracted to him for his honesty, compassion, intelligence and sense of humor. Archie has inspired me more than I can say. He is one of the most selfless people I've met and his story has given others who struggle with learning and reading difficulties hope."

—**Margie Gillis, Ed.D. President, Literacy How, Inc., Research Affiliate Haskins Laboratories**

"It has been our pleasure to work closely with Archie for over seven years to address health literacy with Iowa Health System's Health Literacy Collaborative, and also throughout Iowa and the nation. He still works to improve his reading and is passionate about helping others and continues to work to create a safer, friendlier health delivery system for all especially those who struggle with literacy."

—Mary Ann Abrams, MD, MPH,
Health Literacy Medical Advisor

"Archie Willard has a story to tell that every educator and doctor should read. Archie's true life account of not being able to read in school and early professional life will hit you in the heart. I was captivated by his struggles and the savvy and hard work he used in overcoming them. Archie's voice is authentic and tender; I am touched by his vulnerability and awed by his courage and activism. Archie sharing his story has a profound impact on people; he invites us to be aware that we all have secret shames and are more alike than we sometimes think."

—Terry C. Davis, PhD, Professor, Departments of Medicine and
Pediatrics, Louisiana State University Health Sciences Center

"In the early 1990's, Archie and I were both following a new adult literacy on-line discussion group. He was posting his thoughts on the list used by adult literacy professionals. Now that took some nerve! There were misspellings and wrong words but Archie didn't let that stop him from challenging us to look more deeply into the perspective of the adult learners we served. In both the adult literacy and the health literacy fields, Archie has been an influential presence as he observes our discussions, watches our policies, and contributes a valuable perspective of New Reader and patient. I am so honored to call him my friend and teacher. Archie is a huge inspiration to me, and I'm sure to thousands of other fans."

—Audrey Riffenburgh, MA, Senior Health Literacy Specialist,
University of New Mexico Hospitals

"I met Archie Willard in 1995, at the first meeting of our National Institute for Literacy Research Fellows cohort. Archie's research design was on adult learner leadership and in the years that followed he led adult learner leaders and practitioners to found the Voice of Adult Learners United for Education (VALUE). My colleagues and I across North America very much look forward to reading Archie's autobiography. I am sure we have much to learn from him."

—David J. Rosen, Ed.D, President, Newsome Associates

# LAST READER
# STANDING

## ... The Story of a Man Who Learned to Read at 54

# Archie Willard
## with Colleen Wiemerslage

BETTIE YOUNGS BOOKS

Cover design, Tatomir A. Pitariu
Interior design, Jane Hagaman
Senior Editor, Mark A. Clements
Line Editor, Jazmin Gomez

BETTIE YOUNGS BOOK PUBLISHERS
www.BettieYoungsBooks.com
Info@BettieYoungsBooks.com

If you are unable to order this book from your local bookseller or online from Amazon or Barnes & Noble, or from Espresso or Read How You Want It, you may order directly from the publisher (Sales@ BettieYoungsBooks.com).

ISBN: 978-1-936332-48-9
ePub: 978-1-936332-50-2
Library of Congress Control Number: 2013947505

1. Willard, Archie. 2. Wiemerslage, Colleen. 3. Bettie Youngs Books.
4. Literacy. 5. Reading. 6. Learning. 7. Education. 8. Educators.
9. Childhood Memories. 10. Students. 11. Self-esteem. 12. Dyslexia.
13. Bipolar Disorder. 14. Voting Literacy. 15. Learning Disabilities.
16. Health Literacy. 17. First Lady Barbara Bush.

Printed in the United States of America

# DEDICATION

*I dedicate this book to the memory of my wife Wanda, to my daughter Kelli and my tutor Maxine Thomas. Without them this story wouldn't exist.*

# Table of Contents

## Part Three: Becoming an Advocate

# Foreword

Many people live *interesting* lives; yet we all readily admit that some are more interesting than others. Why do we close some autobiographies with impatience and linger over others? I have to admit that I am drawn to stories that offer me guideposts for my own journey. I am curious about how others actively shape their lives. I am inspired by those who have been able to reflect on their gifts and adversities and then take action based on lessons they learned. You have such a book in hand.

I met Archie Willard many years ago when he invited me to share some of my work related to literacy and health. I was engaged in a new field we called health literacy. Work in this area came about as a result of the National Adult Literacy Survey [published in 1993]. Faced with findings that almost half of US adults have difficulty using print materials with accuracy and consistency, several health researchers asked *"Are there implications for health?"* Research over the last two decades has shown that yes, literacy and health are related. People with limited literacy skills are more likely to face health problems. It was exciting and easy for researchers to get caught up in studies that showed this link.

But Archie, through his participation in conferences and in online discussion groups, insisted that we pay attention to more than just the skills of adults and links to health outcomes. It is important, he insisted, to understand the experiences and insights of the patient. He insisted that we hear the voices of those who have faced difficulty with the written and spoken word and that we pay attention to literacy barriers—to the complex information, to the confusing language, to the maze-like characteristics of health settings. He shared his story to show that insights he developed can help shape better health systems.

My husband, a researcher focused on literacy, knew Archie Willard before me. John Comings told me that Archie played a key role in his field of adult learning as well. Archie, through his work with New Readers, helped educators develop a more positive vision of adult learners and was able to demonstrate how adult learners could serve as great assets to teachers, to researchers, and to policy makers. Archie knew, without necessarily having read pedagogy, that teachers need to hear and understand the experiences of learners so that, together, they can develop solid approaches to teaching and learning. Because of Archie's work with New Readers, adult learners across the country have been advising existing adult education programs and have been advocating for policies and funding in support of adult education.

Archie's voice and vision has made a difference. He has helped adult education programs. He has helped health researchers begin to pay more attention to barriers facing adults as they try to improve their own health, the well-being of loved ones, and the health and safety of their communities.

Archie Willard's story is compelling not merely because he was able to overcome adversity, but because he has been able to draw from his own experiences to take action with and for

others who might otherwise have been silenced and excluded.
Enjoy! I hope that you feel compelled to take action as well.

—Dr. Rima E. Rudd
Department of Society,
Human Development and Health
Harvard School of Public Health

# Acknowledgements

These are people whom I want to mention because of the significance they have had in my growth and leadership: Dr. Mary Ann Abrams, Dr. Paul Beard, Pat Blackwell, Ed Castor, Dale Christianson, Toni Cordell, Dr. Margie Gilles, Nancy Hanson, Andy Hartman, Jane Holbart, Ann Muir, Helen Osborne, Audrey Riffenburgh, Dr. David Rosen, Carmen Schreiber, Marian Temple, and Maxine Thomas.

I want to recognize the direction that Pro-Literacy, and its president and CEO, David C. Harvey, are taking in adult literacy. I also want to recognize VALUE and Marty Finsterbusch, the current executive director, for the leadership programs they continue to develop.

I want to give credit to Margaret Dowdy for the work she is doing by circulating the petition for the Right To Read and to Helen Osborne for the Health Literacy website she has created. The National Coalition and all the literacy organizations that belong to it continue to take positive steps in their fight for literacy. It is important that we support these causes so we can make sure future generations of children will have the opportunity to learn to read.

There are many people who influence us in life whether we have met them or not. In my case the ones I never met but felt great influence from are: Dr. Frank Laubach the founder of Pro Literacy, Miles Horton who is called "the Father of the Civil Rights Movement' for his creation of the Highlander, Dr. Samuel Orton, one of the first researchers of learning disabilities, Elizabeth Cady Stanton and her partner Susan B. Anthony, co-founders of the women's suffrage movement, and Dr. Martin Luther King.

Finally, I want to thank the partnership between the New Readers of Iowa and the Iowa Health System. It's a one-of-a-kind relationship that I am proud to have helped partner. I am very proud of both groups and their work in health literacy.

*Last Reader Standing*

# Preface

## About Archie

I met Archie five years ago as we left a yoga class and ended up walking home together. As we walked, Archie began telling me about one of his theories and "how you need to be open to connections and take advantage of chance encounters."

My new friend Archie told me he did public speaking, was an advocate for literacy and was a "New Reader." Although I'd been an educator for over thirty years I did not know this term, so I asked, "What does being a New Reader mean, Archie?"

He explained that New Readers are people who don't know how to read, at least very well, for a variety of reasons. I was grateful to have a new phrase to replace "illiterate."

I told him I was retired from my full-time job as an educator, which for 35 years spread across a multitude of experiences including teaching first, second and third grades as well as special education, seventh and eighth grade science, followed by the last fifteen years as a high school counselor.

I've always wondered why my teaching career led me down so many paths when many educators keep the same position their entire working life. Of course, many of the changes were the result of being a new employee and simply taking what was offered to me, but the last two positions were my choice. Then

I retired young to spend more time with my husband, children and grandchildren. I also have other professional goals to pursue, such as the family column I write for a newspaper, and the book I'm writing.

The following winter, in February of 2011, I was enjoying coffee with Archie and some other friends when someone enquired about my column. Archie looked at me and said, "I want you to write my book."

"You want me to do what?"

"Well, you're a good writer and I trust you, so I think you should write my book."

That afternoon he and I met to discuss what was only a possibility in my mind but a commitment in Archie's. I soon learned about a man so selfless that I knew I was in the presence of greatness. That only added to my feelings of inadequacy about doing this magnificent man's story justice. I tried to get off the hook but Archie was determined. When I went home and told my husband about Archie and his amazing life, my husband encouraged me to continue.

Although Archie and I live in different states, Wisconsin and Iowa, we both winter in Arizona. This was not an obstacle for Archie. Almost nothing is an obstacle for Archie; he's learned to not let things get in his way. When you get this quiet, accomplished man talking about literacy he's full of passion about where he's been, how far he's come and the current literacy project that has his attention. He's an inspiration for many reasons—but especially because at age 82 he's still making a difference.

Archie is humble—Mother Teresa and Gandhi-type humble. He has so little need for recognition that he never assumes anyone is above approaching about getting involved in his quest. He doesn't overthink or analyze things; he just does them. Everyone he has come to know in his quest for making a difference in the world of literacy loves him and his ideas. I realized I had so much to learn from him . . . so I agreed to write his story.

As you will soon learn, Archie uses spontaneous moments to act as an advocate for individuals who cannot read, while also demonstrating leadership prowess in many literacy arenas. Since I've always been a planner and organizer myself, I was intrigued by his methods and wanted to know more about my new friend.

In the pages that follow you will learn, as I did, what it means to be a "New Reader." You will be inspired by Archie Willard and how he began a new life at the age of 54. And you will be amazed at how he has used his new skills to make a difference in the world of literacy.

—Colleen O'Reilly Wiemerslage B.S., M.S.

# Introduction

*A bird does not sing because it has answers;*
*it sings because it has a song*
*—Chinese Proverb*

As you read my book I want you to keep the following thoughts in mind . . .

There are many people in the world who cannot read well, who have trouble with written and spoken language—and they are being left behind. Their true potential cannot be fulfilled because they lack the skills and confidence to fully explore the world.

I am writing this book because I want people dealing with learning disabilities to find hope and to begin living their lives again. I want to inspire New Readers to accept leadership roles and find their purpose in life. I want to empower the parents of learning-disabled children to advocate on behalf of their kids. And finally, I hope my story will help educators, medical practitioners and others have more compassion and empathy for the learning disabled individuals they serve in their professions.

Einstein, Edison, Churchill, Da Vinci, Hans Christian Anderson and many others had a passion that allowed them to find their ways to success despite disabilities. But not everyone can find their own way. I want my story to provide a voice for the many people with poor literacy skills whose lives have been damaged by their inability to read or read properly. I share my story to create awareness of all those who have not had the opportunity to learn to read as well as of all of us "New Readers." Hopefully this book will inspire educators, medical practitioners and parents to understand the importance of their roles and motivate all people with reading challenges to ask for help and seek answers.

Understanding the root of my reading problems opened my eyes and helped me begin to find my way in life. I began to see beauty in the world that I had never experienced before, and felt the joy of living in a way I had never known before. The challenges for the dyslexic are different every day. If you meet those challenges, you'll discover that each day is a new and beautiful experience. Now that I finally understand this, I fall in love with life all over again every day.

It makes me want to fly.

My book is intended to shed light on a piece of history. I also want to inspire you to take up the cause of literacy as I have, so others who cannot read can find hope.

—Archie Willard, 2013

# Part One

# Archie Marion Willard, Born August 22, 1930

*Giving criticism but not giving a second chance is wrong.*
—Archie Willard

Chapter 1

# Living Proof

## The Unexpected Path

Barbara Bush stepped out on stage before an excited audience and began her speech. The year was 1994—a decade after I'd found out I was dyslexic and finally began to learn to read—and here I was invited to speak along with the First Lady. I was ready for it. I'd logged my speech into my memory and put on my fanciest suit.

Eventually Mrs. Bush stopped speaking, looked my way and invited me to come up on stage. As she shook my hand and introduced me to the audience I felt that I was floating. It was not fear, but excitement. I approached the podium in my $400 suit, blinded by the bright lights and a little apprehensive about the Secret Service and the 2,000 people watching me. I had never spoken to such a large group of people.

As I stood at the lectern I was aware of my heart beating in my throat. I said to myself, *You don't have time to be scared. You need to do this.* So I took a deep breath and began:

"I am dyslexic and I am a New Reader. I'm proud of whom I am and am no longer ashamed of my reading problems. At age

54, I went to an adult reading program to improve my reading. This inspired me to become an advocate for literacy, which is how I came to be a speaker here today. The adult literacy programs in America gave me a second chance in life and continue to do so for many others across this nation. I am living proof of why this program works."

When I finished I was thrilled to receive a standing ovation: me, little old Archie Willard from Eagle Grove, Iowa! I couldn't help but wonder what my primary school teachers—all those who never hesitated to let me know how stupid I was—would think of me now.

Following the speech, my wife Wanda and I walked into the private reception with Mrs. Bush. I still felt like I was not really there. Although I was fully aware of the tables of food and all the other people, I felt that this couldn't really be happening. *This must be what people refer to as an out of body experience*, I thought. I felt as if I were looking down and watching myself attend this event. I wanted to remember every single detail of this most important moment in my life.

Mrs. Bush greeted each person who entered the room, and as she approached Wanda and me I was aware of what an impressive, formidable woman she was. I sensed the energy surrounding her as she moved through the room. It was a power she had obviously learned to use well.

"Archie," she said, "Your speech was wonderful. It's difficult for me to believe you've only recently learned to read. You need to continue spreading the word."

She went on to thank me for speaking with her and I held onto Wanda's hand, uncertain if it was she who was shaking, or me. We looked at each other and smiled.

After Mrs. Bush left, one of her aides came over to talk with us. "I have a connection to your community," she said. "My grandfather was Dr. Elmer Smith, a physician in Eagle Grove."

I smiled. "No kidding. He was the doctor who took care of the football team when I played for Eagle Grove High School."

The aide explained that her father, Bob Smith, grew up in Eagle Grove and also was a physician. "I'm so happy to meet you and Wanda, and my father will love hearing about you. Do you have any football stories he might recall?"

"It was a long time ago," I said. "I'd have to think about it. Perhaps we could talk again sometime."

The next day as I was thinking over the remarkable events of the previous day I realized that if I weren't dyslexic I wouldn't have had the opportunity to be there at all. Barbara Bush had contacted North Iowa Community College seeking an adult learner to speak with her at an Iowa Literacy Fundraiser, and they contacted me. Yes, I'm an adult learner and yes, I've worked very hard to learn to read . . . but I was still amazed that I'd been selected for this honor.

I'll never forget how excited I was when I received the call to speak with Barbara Bush. Wanda and I toasted my good fortune at dinner that night. As I looked across the table at Wanda I realized her eyes were moist. I leaned in and took her hand. "What's the matter, dear? You look so sad."

"I'm so *proud* of you, Archie. My heart is bursting with love. You are such an amazing man and I'm the luckiest woman in the world to have you for my husband."

I was speechless. We sat there holding hands until Wanda broke the silence: "Now we have to decide what we'll buy for you to wear to such an important event."

Two nights before I was to give my speech to the largest and most important audience of my life I received a call from Washington, D.C. Bonita Summerfield, the director of Barbara Bush's Literacy Foundation, wanted to know what I was going to say in my speech. When she asked if she could have a copy I started to panic—I never wrote my speeches out, and was worried they wouldn't want me to speak if I didn' follow protocol. But finally I said, "I don't write out my speeches . . . so could I just tell it to you?"

"Of course."

When I finished she said, "Archie, I've never known anyone who doesn't write out their speeches. I don't understand—how can you remember all of that?"

"I'm dyslexic," I said. "If I write out my speech I won't be able to read it anyway. So I just remember the stories I want to tell, then review the beginning and end of each of them—and I'm ready to go."

"Wow!" she said. "That's amazing. Maybe you should teach other people how to do that."

After we hung up I stood there with the phone in my hand for what seemed like an hour as I thought about what this all meant. I was excited and proud. What an opportunity for me to speak out for literacy.

It was a path no one in my early life would have predicted I would take. . . .

Chapter 2

# School Changes My Life Forever

## Kindergarten, 1935

I grew up in a little house with only two bedrooms but I loved the way it smelled, especially when my mother was baking cinnamon rolls. I always licked the spoon before my sisters could get to it because they didn't want boy germs. As the baby of the family I knew that my sisters were sometimes jealous of me, especially around my dad, who was happy to finally have a boy.

I thought I was a pretty normal kid. My mom stayed home, like most of my friend's mothers. She was a hard worker who kept the peace in our family. My father worked a lot—12 hours a day, every day except for a half day on Sunday. He always told me he was happy he had such a good job with the railroad, although he wished the workers were respected more. I didn't really understand that, but I knew it had to be important for him to tell it to me. He was usually tired from working so much and didn't hear well, so he missed out or misunderstood many of the things I tried to tell him. But he was kind and caring; I knew he loved us and would always protect and take care of us.

Shortly before I started kindergarten my parents added a room to our attic for me. I really liked that I had this big room all to myself. I loved the way the ceiling angled in and how I had to scrunch down as I got closer to the walls. It was like having my own big fort—and best of all I didn't have to share it with my sisters.

My eldest sister Arlene was five years older than me and teased me a lot. Margaret was only two and a half years older but joined in on the teasing. Since they weren't really mean about it I just went along and teased them back. If things happened to escalate into a fight my mother always yelled at the girls, so I knew I wouldn't get in trouble even though I was already taller than Arlene.

One of my favorite things to do with my sisters was to make what we called "ghost tunnels" in the basement by hanging blankets over the clotheslines. We had scary clothes and messages that we made from old pieces of clothing and boxes. If you haven't made ghost tunnels you should try it, especially in the winter when the snow and wind make it too cold to play outside, or in the deepest heat of summer.

My mother let us invite the neighborhood friends over, and we'd make them walk through the ghost tunnels so we could scare them. They knew what we were doing, of course, but they got scared anyway. Once we even scared the meter man when he went into the basement to check the meter. My mother was kind of embarrassed by that, but my sisters and I couldn't stop laughing.

I liked being home alone with Mom because she helped me learn to count to 100. I was really good at counting, and also at coloring. I knew all my nursery rhymes. I was excited to start kindergarten at Lincoln Elementary in the fall so I could be in the same school that my sisters went to every day. Everyone expected that I would be a good student, just like my sisters. I certainly knew I was smart. None of my friends knew how to count to 100.

We had to bring a rug to school for nap time. I never fell asleep on mine, but some kids did and my friends and I giggled because they snored. My teacher, Miss Paterson, was very young and beautiful and kind to all of us. I got up very early every day so I'd be ready to go before everyone else. I couldn't wait to get to school.

As the kindergarten year wound to its end the first grade teacher took each one of us aside and showed us pictures and asked us questions to see if we were ready for first grade. I answered every question and was proud and excited that I did so well.

I couldn't wait for first grade to start.

## First Grade, 1936

"Archie," my mother said, "you walk to school with your sisters." Of course, my sisters refused to walk with me because they wanted to be with their friends. I didn't care because pretty soon I was walking with my friends too. Not that it was much of a walk: the school—a big two-story orange brick building—was only four blocks away from my house.

Unfortunately, the walk turned out to be the only thing easy about first grade. In fact first grade changed my life forever, but not in the way I had hoped. My initial excitement at being in grade school soon began to fade as I realized I was different from the other kids. Because I had done so well in kindergarten, my first grade teacher, Miss Anderson, put me immediately in the A group . . . but when she realized I couldn't read the words she presented me, she moved me straight down to the bottom of the class.

I was shocked. What was wrong with me? The other kids were able to put sounds together to figure out new words, but I just couldn't make the sounds blend together. I felt stupid. Worse, I felt terrified: When I looked down at my books, the words were a blur. My mind raced out of control; my heart beat faster and faster.

Whenever the teacher called on me to read I felt like I was on a stage and didn't know my lines. The kids looked at me funny and a sick feeling in my stomach made me feel scared and alone. I wouldn't look at anyone. I didn't want anyone to know that I couldn't read the words. I didn't want anyone to know what a bad student I was. I was a failure. I wished I could just disappear.

When Miss Anderson put me in the back of the classroom my shame deepened. She kept all the good students up front by her; the worse a student you were, the farther back in the room you were seated. No one's desk was farther from Miss Anderson's than mine. It wasn't that she was being particularly mean; she just didn't have any patience with a kid who seemed unable or, worse, *unwilling* to learn.

Every minute of every day I sat in the back of the room terrified that Miss Anderson would call on me to read. I scooted down in my chair and hoped to not be noticed. This turned out to be a wasted effort because she never did call on me; she ignored me. I didn't tell my sisters or my Mom or Dad about any of this because I didn't want them to know I was a bad student. I was so ashamed. I felt that I was doing something wrong.

After lunch we had penmanship class. In those days we used steel-tipped pens and the desks had inkwells in them. The inkwells were on the right side for the convenience of most students, who are right-handed—but I'm a lefty, so every time I dipped my pen in the ink and brought it back to the paper my sleeve dragged through the well and smeared everything. A girl named Connie and I were the only left-handers in our class. One day Miss Anderson snapped, "Archie and Connie, you're making a mess. I'm moving you into the coatroom until you do better."

The coatroom was a terrible place to be, but I was too frightened to tell the teacher that we couldn't hear a thing she said in the classroom. So Connie and I just sat there wasting time. Worse, the coatroom was unheated, and by December we were miserable in that refrigerator. Still, I didn't tell my parents because that would mean explaining why I'd been exiled to the Siberia of the coatroom.

Connie, on the other hand, was brave. One day she told Miss Anderson "It's cold in here and Archie and I don't want to sit here anymore."

"Well, then you can come back into the classroom," Miss Anderson said. That was a relief, except that my dread of the cold turned into fear of making another mess. To calm myself I used my imagination, putting myself into another world where I could read well and had a lot of friends. If the teacher walked by me or yelled at me, I'd check back in long enough to see if I was in real trouble; if not, I'd return to the story inside my head.

Not surprisingly, I soon hated school. Hated Mondays. Halfway through the despised ten-minute walk I'd look ahead at the orange brick building and wanted to either run away or throw up. As I walked through the halls I'd hang my head. None of the kids talked to me. I felt as if I were on that floodlit stage. All my intentions to be a really good student were gone.

My parents soon figured out I was having trouble in school but they just told me to "do my best." Although they worked hard they didn't have a lot of education themselves; all they wanted for me was that I also work hard too, and be healthy.

For my part I wanted to do my best but I was afraid to try, afraid to fail. I preferred to stay at home with my mother and father and sisters, because home was safe and comfortable.

Chapter 3

# I Hate School

## 1938-1945

Every year of grade school it was the same thing: I was made to sit in the back of the room, where I looked out the window and watched the leaves change color, the snowflakes fall and the trees return to leaf. I longed for spring because it gave me hope. Summer would give me a break from the painful daily grind of not being able to read what all my classmates were reading and learn what they were learning.

I was constantly anxious and spent every school day trying to avoid situations that might make me feel even more stupid or embarrassed than I already was. My handwriting was terrible; so even when I did work on assignments the teacher couldn't read the parts I managed to finish. I was a good math student—except when I copied problems down wrong. My report cards had a lot of F's on them, although by the end of the year I ended up with some D's. I sure was glad my parents didn't get mad at me or blame me for being such a bad student. They seemed to understand that I was doing the best I could.

During class I tried to be quiet and not cause trouble so no one would notice me, but I felt that my teachers were waiting for me to do something wrong. All I had to do was turn in my seat and they'd attack me: "Archie, sit still and be quiet!"

I didn't know what I was doing to make them treat me that way. I didn't know why I couldn't read like the other kids, but why did the teachers have to make me feel that it was my fault? That they blamed me for being stupid. They were old, so maybe they thought I was like bad kids they'd had before, and didn't want me to get out of control. The truth was I was not a bad kid, I just couldn't read.

In 1940, when I was a fourth grader, my teacher, Miss Fischer, tried to get me caught up. She kept me after school every night. Although other kids had to stay and work with her too, I was the worst reader. Still, I found ways to get by. Miss Fischer would work with the other kids first, so by the time she got around to me I knew everything she was going to ask, and what the proper answers were.

Still, oh how I hated staying after school. It was bad enough to be in that place all day long, but to be kept afterward for an extra hour—sometimes two–every day? Like any other kid, all I wanted to do was get outside and play with my neighborhood friends, but I was always the last to leave. Why was I was the only kid like this? How come nobody else had this problem?

I had developed an attitude toward mean teachers, but I started to think that maybe Miss Fischer really cared about me. She seemed to honestly want to help me do better. She never seemed unkind; she just made me work harder than anyone else. And I did work for her—but when teachers were mean I just gave up.

The one thing I didn't do was let anyone—not Miss Fischer, not my friends, not even my family—understand how deep and fundamental my underlying problem was: I couldn't read. I couldn't make sense of the words on the page. Everyone else my age could read just fine, so I wasn't going to let anyone see my true weakness. Instead I showed people my strong points so they wouldn't make fun of me. I'm sure my parents suspected the truth, but they never asked me to read anything and we didn't talk about my learning problems. Most likely they just didn't know what to do with me so, they simply loved and supported me as long as I did my best.

Unlike most kids, I hated recess as much as I hated the rest of school. Most of the time my classmates ignored me, but at recess some of them made fun of me. I tried to stay away from them, but had nowhere to go. One day two kids kept calling me stupid and telling me I belonged in kindergarten. They wouldn't stop, even when I ignored them. Finally I got so mad and embarrassed that I fought back, screaming and swinging my fists.

One of the teachers on the playground took us all to the principal's office. I had never been there before, and didn't want to be there. The principal showed me a rubber hose and told me she'd use it on me if I continued to get into trouble. The teacher had told her that I'd been getting into fights with a lot of different kids, which made the principal think I was the troublemaker. I was scared but at the same time furious that she didn't even try to change her mind.

After I saw that rubber hose I started spending my recesses sitting on the steps on the other side of the building, away from everybody.

I lived for the weekends. Every Saturday I played football with my neighborhood friends. On Sunday my dad would read to me before he left for work. My Mom didn't read very well herself, so she never read me a story. I always looked forward to whatever book Dad shared with me. Home was safe; it was only at school that I felt stupid.

## Football

I had lots of friends in my neighborhood because the kids there were older than me and didn't know how I was treated by my classmates, or that I couldn't read. One of the boys, Bill, liked how I played football and challenged me to play harder.

One day in the fall the boys in my fifth grade class asked me to play football with them against the sixth grade boys. I couldn't believe it. This was the first time they ever asked me to play with them. Someone on the fifth grade team must have heard about my neighborhood games with the older kids. I was so excited I could hardly believe it. All that Saturday football was paying off.

The game was held after school, and for once I got to show off. I think some of the kids could hardly believe how fast I ran how well I executed plays. Although we lost the game, nobody blamed me. Even better, after that day things got better with my classmates; they even started to invite me to hang out with them at school.

Despite this, fifth grade was my most challenging year of school because one of my teachers, Miss Brooks, wouldn't even talk to me. To punish me for poor penmanship she smacked my knuckles with a ruler. "You're so messy, you're getting ink all over the table!"

Although I didn't hate anyone, I thought really bad thoughts when Miss Brooks got near me, and especially when she hit me. She broke three rulers across my hand before my mother found out and came to school to talk to the principal. I was never hit with a ruler again.

Still, the worst news was that Miss Brooks was my spelling and math teacher all the way through eighth grade. One time in math—my best subject—I raised my hand to give an answer and she said, in front of the entire class, "You're lying, Archie. I don't believe you really know the answer, so from now on I will not call on you."

I was so angry I felt like I was going to explode. I thought more bad things about her, but tried not to let it show on my face because I didn't want her to yell at me again. Apparently she thought I was just raising my hand to be like the other kids and not because I really knew the answers. What was the use of even trying in her classes? I gave up.

Unfortunately this became a recurring theme in my school life. For example, one day we were practicing for a Christmas program, all the fifth and sixth grade kids together. My sisters and I took music lessons from our neighbor, so I was a pretty good singer, and got picked to move to the front. Miss Christianson, one of the teachers, was helping with the rehearsal that day, and singled me out for abuse. "I thought you were supposed to be able to sing in tune," she said. I was so embarrassed that I just stopped singing.

WWII started when I was in fifth grade. I listened to everything on the radio about the war because I wanted to know about the planes and places and events. It was kind of funny, but as the days went by I noticed how much more I knew about the war than my friends and classmates did. It seemed strange to me that people who could read didn't know as much about the people, places and equipment as I did.

I had a constant little battle within myself about whether or not I was as dumb as my teachers made me think I was. How could I know all this stuff about the war and still be stupid? I hoped it meant something good for me, but I didn't know who to ask. Like I said, we never talked about my problems at home and my Mom and Dad never criticized or yelled at me about school. They just said, "Archie, do the best you can." And I would, provided my teacher was nice to me. When I got embarrassed I stopped working.

In eighth grade we had a new principal, Mr. Anderson, who moved me to his class for spelling. Miss Brooks had probably told him I didn't do any work in her class, that I didn't even write things down. I'd given up a long time ago with her, but I kind of liked working with Mr. Anderson. I started to feel that I could trust him so I applied myself and did better.

On top of that, on the very first day of eighth grade I walked into Miss McIlwane's room and sat in the back as always. She saw me do this and I waited for her to yell at me.

Instead, when she finally talked to me she said, "You come up here by me, Archie." She didn't say it in a commanding voice, just as a request. After class she explained to me privately, "I know you have a hard time with school, Archie, but in my class you're going to be in the front of the room and I'm going to help you learn as much as you can."

Wow, she really cared about me, and didn't make fun of me for not being able to read. Even though I was not a very good student, she tried to help me—and, as always, this made me want to do my best.

Chapter 4

# I Got My Free Malts

## Eagle Grove High School

My friend George said, "Hey Archie, I have to go to my tuba lesson. Why don't you come along and then afterwards we can go right to the pool to swim?"

It was the summer before I'd be starting high school, and I didn't really want to go with him to his lesson—but if it meant we could get to the pool sooner, I was more than willing.

After my friend's lesson the instructor handed me the tuba and said, "Play me some notes, Archie." This became a tradition. Every week I'd go with George to his lesson and play a few notes; so you could say I took some tuba lessons.

I was 15 when I started high school in 1945. World War II had just ended. I had learned to trust my "wait and see" method of dealing with new situations, but I also knew that high school would present many new obstacles for me. Just thinking about all the unfamiliar teachers, textbooks, assignments and tests I would face filled me with mixed enthusiasm and fear. I had butterflies in my stomach because I didn't know what to expect.

"You're a fast runner, Archie," my 8th grade PE teacher had told me at the end of the previous school year. "You should be out there playing football." Maybe this would be my way to acceptance in high school. I'd heard that the high school was issuing football uniforms, so I headed over to the school and picked one up. Although the freshmen practiced with all the grades, we weren't allowed to make the varsity team. I didn't care. I was good at playing end on both offense and defense, and was proud to be able to do something well. I might not be able to play with the varsity team until my junior year, but the freshman and sophomores played one another a lot, which was great fun and gave us plenty of practice.

As I had expected, the first day of high school was both scary and exciting. To my surprise, as I walked into the building a bunch of kids came running up to me and yelled, "Hey Archie, your name is on the list to be in band!"

"It is?" I said. Sure enough, they needed another tuba player, and the band instructor believed I could manage because of the lessons I'd had during the summer." Between being in the band and playing football I was actually excited about going to school.

Kids entering high school in Eagle Grove came from small country schools as well as the various schools in town. This mixture gave me a new chance to find my place because so many of the kids had not seen me fail in grade school. As a result, high school was better than the previous eight years of school combined. I was well accepted by most teachers and students. The teachers for the most part were very respectful, which changed my attitude toward school. I wasn't made fun of and didn't have to sit in the back of the class. I'd always wanted to be accepted, and it was finally beginning to happen.

The problem was, I still couldn't read. I'd memorized enough words to help me get by, but I couldn't read the textbooks. I just listened and learned what I could during class.

By then my sisters were married and busy with their own lives, so they didn't have time to help me study. My dad worked a lot, and my mother had reading troubles of her own. Although we didn't talk about it, I knew she had a hard time. And she wasn't the only one. She told me that my grandpa signed his name with an X.

Still, I managed to get through my classes and turn in my homework—with a little help from my friends. For me, schooling was like playing football: I needed to work with others to be successful. I don't mean by cheating, and I don't mean I became a great student. My grades were mostly C's and D's, and I got very worried when semester test time rolled around. I could only hope that my day-to-day work would make up for my lack of success on the tests. For the most part my teachers seemed to appreciate that I was doing the best I could, and probably nudged my grades accordingly.

## President Archie

In my sophomore year, after the first week of classes, we met in the auditorium to nominate class officers. I was shocked when several people nominated me for class president. I felt honored and also wanted to see if I could do it, so I accepted the nomination.

Even during the worst of times in my life there has always been a little voice inside me that says, "Don't be afraid, just do it"—so I did. When the election was held I won. It felt so good to be appreciated. *Hopefully I won't let them down.*

I asked the advisor what my responsibilities would be, and she told me that I would mostly be organizing and planning events. My nervousness eased a bit. Our class went on to take first place in many events that year, such as Best Homecoming Float and first place in the pep skit. Although these successes were a direct reflection of the enthusiastic people we had in our class, the fact that they came during my period of leadership gave me confidence.

On the other hand, my varsity football coach was a hot-head I didn't like playing for. The anger and severe discipline he showed towards us players reminded me of my early elementary school teachers. Whenever he pulled me out of a game he'd send me to the end of the bench, where I felt like I was being forced to sit in the rear of the room all over again. It made me not try as hard as I normally did, as much as I loved playing football.

During my senior year we got a new coach, Coach Savage. He had a better way of working with us, and for him I did my best. He only pulled me out of a game once, and when he did it he didn't yell at me—he just put his arm around my shoulder and said, "You can do better than that, Archie. I believe in you," and sent me back into the game.

I played my best game at Homecoming that year. Although Mom often came to my games, my Dad usually had to work. This time he made it to the game because one of our neighbors gave him a ride after work. I didn't even know he was out there, nor did my Mom. But later he told me how impressed he was with how hard I hit this one guy. Even though my father was hard of hearing, he said he heard the *crack* of the impact. He was proud of me for trying so hard.

A local soda fountain owner and pharmacist, Marv Franzen, told Coach Savage who he thought were the best backfield and lineman for each game, and awarded the winners a free malt. I got free malts five out of the eight games we played that year. Football gave me a reason to stay in high school and graduate at a time when many kids gave up, dropped out and went to work.

I ended up staying in band all the way through high school. Interestingly, I found reading music much easier than reading words. I loved all the places and experiences we had. We marched in a lot of parades and even got invited to march at the Drake University relays as well as Homecoming at Iowa State University. Being in the band really got my juices going and made me get excited about being in school. I was happy to do something that made me feel important and successful.

At Senior Awards Day I found out I had been awarded a football scholarship to Eagle Grove Community College. I'd never thought football would open doors for me. Although I was proud of this honor, I knew I'd have to do the schoolwork as well, and didn't know if I would be able to study at a college level.

Of course, my parents were happy for me and encouraged me to "do my best."

## Eagle Grove Community College

It was 1949 when I started classes at Eagle Grove Community College. Being on the football team was great and I did very well at it, but I struggled more than ever before to get good grades. I didn't have much time for socializing, either, because I had to study so hard to stay eligible for football.

Junior college was much more difficult than high school and I didn't have as much help. Most of my fellow students were older than I, using their GI benefits and busy with family and studies. They'd been out of school for a few years so they had to work hard to get good grades themselves; I couldn't expect them to spend time helping me.

With my old techniques from high school unavailable to me, I needed to develop new study skills. I chose to depend on my memory. I listened intently to lectures in class, then returned to my room at home and reviewed the lectures in my brain. I went over and over them until I felt I had the information locked into memory.

One of my classes was Government. One day the teacher forgot to mimeograph off copies of the test, so he said, "Heck, since it's too late to go run this off I might as well just read it to the whole class."

The test was multiple choice, so all I had to do was listen and write down the letter of the answer I selected. I got the third highest score in class. No doubt I would have done better in all my classes if I'd had the tests read aloud to me. One unexpected gift of not being able to read is the ability to listen and remember with a clarity I seldom see in others. It allowed me to graduate from high school and attend college. At the time I didn't know what this situation revealed about my brain, but I hoped it was something good.

I managed to make it through the two years of junior college, and to my surprise got three offers to play football at small four-year colleges. I decided to attend Buena Vista College, but again worried that the studies would be too much for me. This time my fears were justified; memory tricks and hard work were not enough. It didn't take long for me realize I couldn't get my grades up high enough to remain eligible for football. I didn't want to tell anyone I needed help, and didn't know who I'd tell anyway. So I decided it was time for me to drop out of college, find a job and go to work. Perhaps someday I'd manage to go back to college, where I'd earn an education degree in history or social studies, and of course be a coach, too.

But as it turned out, that wouldn't be my dream after all.

Part Two

# Archie as an Adult

*Learn From Yesterday,*
*Live for Today and*
*Hope for Tomorrow.*
*—Albert Einstein*

## Chapter 5

# Feeling A Nobody

Since I couldn't continue with my college plans I knew I had to find a job, and in 1951 I started working for the Hormel Meat packing plant in Fort Dodge, Iowa. Although I had higher aspirations for myself, I didn't know how I could fulfill them. To work at Hormel I didn't need to know how to read; I just had to be fast with my hands. I guess you could say I kind of gave up again. As a teacher I would have been somebody special in my community, but working at the plant made me feel like a nobody.

Not that it was all bad. In fact as far as labor jobs go it was fine; the wages and benefits were good and the company was fair to its employees. The down side was that there was nothing to look forward to each day, because you always did the same thing.

My work day started at 7AM and ran until 4PM. I got three breaks: 15 minutes in the morning, 30 minutes for lunch, and 15 more minutes in the afternoon. The rest of the time I stood in the same position close to the same three people and did the same task over and over again, processing pig heads to remove the cheek and jaw meat, the "pork cutlets." It was repetitive, boring work. It felt like a waste of my life.

Before long I knew everything and more about the three people I worked next to. I knew their likes, dislikes, their children's problems; I knew all about their marriages and their parents. I felt that I should have something more to do, but didn't know what it might be since I couldn't read.

As I looked around the plant I realized there were a lot of people there in the same boat as me. Like me, they seemed frustrated by their lots in life; even those who had never worked anywhere else. Still, they were proud of their work.

A lot of my fellow employees were heavy drinkers who, after their shifts ended, went straight to the bar behind the plant. It was a big deal to see who could get to the tavern first. I occasionally stopped for a beer to be social, but mostly I just headed home—back to the same house I grew up in. My dad had passed away and my mother had moved to Sioux City to work in the hospital, so I now lived in the old place alone.

Since I was starting my job at the bottom of the ladder, my vacation options were limited: in fact, my only choice was February. At lunch I asked the guys sitting around the table, "What's a single guy going to do for vacation in February?"

"I'd go to Texas," one guy said. So I did.

I drove down alone, and found out it was possible to fly from there to Acapulco, Mexico, for only $35. So the following winter I convinced some friends to go with me, and we drove to Laredo, Texas and took a flight to Acapulco. The stewardesses were staying at the same hotel as us, so we shared a cab with them and even spent some beach time together . . . until the swarthy, charming Mexican men worked their way onto the blankets of our stewardess friends.

One Mexican guy came over and told me to be patient. "Wait

until the Mexican girls see you white guys on the beach. They'll be all over your blankets." Sure enough, along came this cute little Mexican girl, and we hit it off.

For the next three winters I traveled back to Acapulco and enjoyed the same girl's company. I even met her family. It was a pretty grand adventure for a young guy like me. I'd never travelled growing up, so it took guts for me to take such big vacations. It helped that all the married guys at the plant were jealous that us single guys were able to head down to sunny Mexico each winter. Of course we probably made the stories of our adventures sound a little better than they actually were . . . .

Chapter 6

# Tired of Rejection

## Disengaged

Although I enjoyed myself socially at this time of my life I endured some tough losses as well. I'd joined the National Guard and attended summer training at Camp Ripley in Minnesota. There a friend and I met some girls, and I hit it off with one named Marylis. After I returned to Iowa she and I travelled back and forth to spend time together even though she lived in St. Paul. I liked her more and more and her parents really liked me, so it was natural that I asked her to marry me. The year was 1959, and I was excited to be engaged and looked forward to a future together.

I don't really know what happened. Marylis and I never talked about it, but we began to drift apart, and soon the engagement ended.

I tried to move on, but found that going to Lake Okoboji and partying with people every weekend was getting old. I talked with my friend Mike who lived in Minneapolis, and he suggested I get a change of scenery by coming to visit him. He set up a blind date for me, and Susan and I really hit it off. In 1963 we got engaged, with a wedding planned in four months' time.

But there were three problems. First, this was another long distance relationship with all the usual stresses of that. Second, Susan was a flight attendant whose unpredictable work schedule rarely matched up with my Monday through Friday job. But the third problem was the worst one, an old nemesis: I couldn't read or write.

During the long periods when we were apart Susan wrote me letters, and of course she wanted me to write back—especially now that we were engaged and making wedding plans. These were exciting things, things she wanted to share with me, but I avoided writing back because I was afraid that my poor spelling and grammar would give away my terrible secret. Of course it wasn't very honest of me to not share my challenges with her if I wanted our relationship to grow, and I knew that. I had an ongoing debate with myself about how to proceed.

Susan was, of course, upset with me for not writing back. Finally I ran out of excuses and set to work on a letter. I had to do it on my own because this was a love letter; not something I could ask for help with.

As I kept messing up and starting over again I recalled my 8th grade teacher's comment: "Archie, if you don't improve your spelling you're going to have a romance with a beautiful woman some day and it won't work out because you spell so poorly."

I re-wrote the letter at least 20 times before I finally sent it. As my hand released the envelope into the mail slot I thought, *Here goes nothing.*

Sure enough, my relationship with Susan immediately began to deteriorate. Although I don't blame my poor writing skills alone, I'm sure she noticed them. She never said anything, but it had to affect how she felt about me. I also assume she didn't like the idea of leaving the big city to move to a little town in Iowa. On the other hand I couldn't even think about leaving my job at Hormel and moving up to Minneapolis, because that would mean having to apply for jobs—and I couldn't read the applications.

The bottom line was that although both of my engagements ended for various reasons, my reading disability was always one of them. If nothing else, it took some maneuvering for me to simply keep the fact that I couldn't read a secret.

The breakup with Susan was especially painful for me, and took a lot more time to get over. Once again, I was reminded of the opportunities I was losing out on because of my inability to read and write—but I didn't know how to change the situation. My way of coping was to just put it out of my mind.

I was tired of rejection, so I decided to just live my life and not worry about having a wife or even a relationship. I'd live each day as it came and not worry about tomorrow. So on summer weekends I once again headed out to Lake Okoboji with my bachelor friends. Lots of beautiful women were always coming there for a vacation, so we had lots of party opportunities. Then, come winter I'd fly off to Mexico. Overall, the bachelor life felt pretty good to me.

But the pleasure didn't last forever. After a few years I began to feel low about not having anyone close to me. I guess you could say I'd become ready to have a wife and begin the next phase of my life—but I felt stymied by the fact that I still couldn't read, the liability that kept ruining my dreams. I started to get down on myself again. I didn't know how to help myself because I had no more understanding of why I couldn't read than I'd had in first grade.

# Meeting the Love of My Life

Around this time a female friend of mine invited me to a local bar to have a drink. We'd dated a bit in the past but ended up as just good friends, and in fact were both dealing with breakups. As we sat in the bar "crying in our beers" together, some girls she knew came in. She introduced me and they joined us for a drink.

I kind of hit it off with one of the girls, Wanda. She wasn't a knockout or a fancy dresser like my past girlfriends, but that was fine with me. She seemed to be something else: an attractive, average-sized woman with light skin and brown hair. She was pretty, but her beauty wasn't sophisticated but homespun and warm, and she seemed genuinely kind and sincere. And the best news: I could tell she was interested in me.

Even so, I wasn't sure I wanted to get involved again. How could I be sure any woman would accept an adult man who couldn't read or write? Not wanting another broken heart, I waited a couple of weeks before I gave in and called Wanda to invite her on a date.

I was very cautious about my feelings towards her because I didn't want to relive the past. On the one hand I didn't want to lead her on; on the other hand I feared opening myself up to falling for her. I was still hanging out with my buddies on weekends at Lake Okoboji because Wanda and I weren't really an item. We were kind of just friends who enjoyed each other's company . . . but bit by bit I began to realize that neither of us was looking at other people or dating anyone else. We were growing together. It surprised me when I realized how attracted I was to Wanda. I guess you could say we became really good friends before we became lovers.

The moment I realized I was in love with this woman and wanted to marry her was terrifically romantic: We were standing in the Laundromat while she washed my clothes. I had been paying two older ladies to do my laundry, but they were going to be gone for two weeks and as I was driving to Wanda's house with my trunk full of dirty clothes I'd wondered if it was appropriate to ask her to help me with my laundry.

After I worried about it for a while I finally just asked her and she said, "I'm more than willing to help you, Archie." Years later we laughed about my trunk full of dirty laundry.

After three years of dating I asked Wanda to marry me. I'd bought the ring a couple of months earlier, then looked around for the right moment in our lives.

We went to a movie and when I drove her back to her house I just pulled out the ring, took Wanda's hand as I said, "Wanda, I love you very much and it would make me so happy if you would be my wife."

At first she was somewhat bewildered; we'd already been together for so long I think she was sure I would never ask her. Then she looked at me and said, "Archie, I would be so happy to be your wife."

Wanda was so accepting of me. She never pressured me; she just enjoyed our time together. She was kind of bashful but so kind too and thoughtful of others. I was such a lucky guy;I could hardly believe my good fortune. In three years of knowing Wanda she had been a loving and supportive friend and now we were in love and looking forward to spending our lives together.

Still, as with my previous relationships, I did not talk about my limitations—and Wanda never asked. I guess you could say that I was still not willing to tell *anyone* about my reading problem because I didn't see a purpose to it. Telling Wanda would only humiliate me and would not improve our relationship.

I invited her on a little vacation to visit a friend of mine who was attending Mankato State College in Mankato, Minnesota. While we were enjoying our weekend together we told him and his wife that we were engaged to be married. We mentioned that because Wanda's parents and my father had already passed away we'd have to put on our own wedding.

Our friends said, "Why don't you come over here and get married?"

I thought about that. If we got married in Iowa there would be a waiting period along with a blood test, and we wanted to avoid the cost. A lot of people were going to other states to get married, so we thought, Why not? We didn't have a lot of family, so why do the big wedding with tuxes and cake and a party? We'd rather use our money to buy furniture and other things we needed.

After considering the possibilities we decided it was less expensive and more practical to go to St. Peter, Minnesota. We drove back the following weekend and got married, on April 2, 1966. We invited another couple from Minneapolis who stood up for us because I'd been the best man in their wedding.

Only six people were in that great big church, but it was our special day. I had on a suit and Wanda was wearing a pretty new light blue dress she bought for the occasion. She looked so special and I was excited to be standing there with her. I kept asking myself, *Am I good enough to be the husband Wanda deserves? Is this really happening?* After years of heartbreak with my other relationships it was difficult to believe I was actually saying my vows to this wonderful woman.

After the ceremony we drove to Minneapolis with the other

two couples and had dinner at a restaurant recommended by our Mankato friends. After we were seated my best man, Dick, raised his glass and said, "Here's a toast to Archie and Wanda. May they enjoy a long and healthy life together."

We all clinked our glasses. Again I couldn't believe I was sitting there with Wanda and we were married. I wasn't afraid of the future because I knew that Wanda would never criticize me or leave me just because I couldn't read or write. Although she didn't know about my challenges, over the three years of our relationship she had most likely noticed things and wondered what they meant,but she had never challenged or questioned. I was so grateful to have found such a loving partner. This was exactly what I needed, to have hope again.

Our honeymoon consisted of one night at a motel and driving back to Iowa the next day. That may sound ordinary, but it was a big change for both of us. We now had different obligations to each other.

As we drove home we talked about the big honeymoon trip to Mexico we'd take later.

## Meeting My Daughter

My life was changing rapidly, going from a single man who traveled to Acapulco every winter to getting married and then expecting a child. My first thought when I found out Wanda was pregnant was *I'm not good enough to be a father*. During the pregnancy I thought often about how I, like my mother, would be unable to read a book to my child. But I knew that Wanda would, so our child would be fine in that respect. For my part, I reminded myself how my father had loved me and always been there for me; I could do the same for my child.

Before the birth Wanda and I moved out of my family home into a two and a half bedroom ranch-style house with a nice lot, right in town. We were there watching *Batman* on TV when Wanda began to have labor pains. She said, "I want to see the end of this before we go to the hospital."

"What? But—there's—we've never even watched *Batman* before!"

"I want to watch the rest anyway."

I think she was just trying to keep us from going to the hospital too soon. When we finally got there they took her to a room and told me to go downstairs to fill out some paperwork. I was so worried about Wanda and the baby that it didn't occur to me to panic about reading and filling out the paperwork, but still, when it was over the admissions people clearly sensed my anxiety and gave me an escort back to the maternity ward.

Once Wanda was ready to deliver the baby the nurses sent me to a waiting room. Those were some long, anguishing moments while I waited to meet my child. I was worried about Wanda because I knew that women could die in childbirth and so I had all kinds of mixed feelings as a husband and soon-to-be father.

Our daughter Kelli was born on November 3, 1967. When I first saw her she hadn't been cleaned up yet, and I thought, *They were too rough with her*. I was already being overprotective, like my own dad. When I got up each morning the first thing I did was check on Kelli. I worried that she wasn't breathing. I had no idea what sort of changes this child would bring to my life, but whatever they were, I'd be there for her.

My little girl began to talk before she could walk; she soon had a large vocabulary. Wanda stayed home with her full-time. Wanda had quit her job when she was eight months pregnant;

only after Kelli was a year old did Wanda start to look for a part-time job.

## Honeymoon in Cozumel

On one of my winter trips to Acapulco I had met a couple with whom I stayed in touch over the years. The man was French Canadian and his wife Italian, but they lived in New Mexico full-time. Wanda and I were planning our long-awaited honeymoon, so I called the couple to see if we could meet up. Fortunately, Kelli's daycare sitter was happy to keep her during the week we'd be gone. We flew into Mexico City and my friends met us and took us around to see the sights. We made plans to fly together to Cozumel, a new resort area, because Acapulco had gotten too expensive.

Poor Wanda. She'd never flown before and was not real excited about getting on a second plane so soon. But the flight to Cozumel was short and I reminded her that very soon we'd be sitting on the beach enjoying the water and sun. She grabbed my hand and held on for dear life until the wheels touched down.

Technically there were only three hotels on the beach, so it was very relaxing. We just luxuriated in the sun and sand. We spent some time with my friends and one night played cards with them and another couple they knew, but most of the time we just enjoyed each other.

Our friends wanted us to rent motorcycles and drive around the island. "Wanda," I said, "what do you think?"

"I don't know, Archie. Have you ever driven a motorcycle?"

"Well, no, but I'm sure I can manage." And I did. We had a wonderful time riding the seven miles around the island.

# Watching My Daughter Grow

Until Kelli started first grade I worried that she might turn out to have my reading problems. I held my breath as she began to learn the sounds of letters and started to read words. But as soon as I saw her doing all this in grand fashion I relaxed. She would be okay.

I felt bad that I never read any books to Kelli, but knew I'd stumble over the words. Wanda later told me that this was when she first started to wonder about my reading skills. She knew how important my daughter was to me and was surprised that when Kelli asked me to read to her I would tell her to ask her mother.

Although Kelli ended up being our only child, there were two girls across the street that Kelli was very good friends with and rode to school with every day. One day the other girls' mother said to Kelli, "Why do you get here early every day, Kelli?"

Kelli smiled. "I don't have a sister to fight with, so I enjoy hearing Raydeen and Linda fight when they're getting ready." You could say she found her own way to have sisters.

When Kelli was in third grade I saw a pamphlet at work about bringing a foreign exchange student into your home. I brought an application home and told Wanda, "I think this will be a great opportunity for Kelli. What do you think?"

Wanda hesitated only a moment. "I think you're right; it would be a good experience for all of us. Do you want me to fill this out?"

That was my Wanda: always supportive and willing, and not expecting me to do the written things we needed to take care of.

Our exchange student, Nora, was from Venezuela. She was a textbook example of an exchange student. Everyone in the community loved her, and she was a joy to have in our lives for her senior year in high school. We stayed in touch for a long time after that year and eventually learned that she had graduated from an American college. She went on to earn a Ph.D. and eventually became a professor at the University of Caracas in Venezuela.

The years went by quickly. I continued to work at Hormel while Wanda worked for a local trucking company just down the street. Kelli was in high school, where she was active in music and played the trumpet.

One day Kelli said to me, "You know, Dad, I've tried out some sports but I'm just not good at it like you were. I love my music so I think I'll focus on that."

"That's just fine, Kelli. I'm really proud of you for the excellent student and musician you've become. You don't have to like sports. You have plenty to be proud of without that." I guess she made a good decision. She stayed with her music and was named 2nd Chair at State, with her trumpet.

At Kelli's high school graduation she was named Salutatorian. She was accepted to the University of Iowa, where she would also be in the marching band. I realized Kelli was more like me—more outgoing, not so introverted as her mom. On the other hand, I was grateful that she was smart like her Mother, or like I would like to have been if I could read. The point was that unlike me, Kelli would be able to follow her dreams.

Chapter 7

# Listening to the Voice

## Accepting the Challenge

My friend Daryl Watts talked me into going to a city council meeting to share our concerns about some issues regarding street repair and snow removal. Even though I wasn't that hyped up about the issues, I wanted to see how the council worked.

After watching the meeting I was surprised at how simple the process appeared to be. I told Daryl, "You should run for mayor since you have such a keen interest in city government."

"I will," he said, "if you run for city council."

"No, I don't think so . . . ."

But later that little voice began to challenge me: *Don't be afraid, just do it.* I thought, *It wouldn't be that hard.* I wanted to see if I could do it. I also needed something extra in my life because my job didn't allow me to grow. I guess you could say I was bored.

So I ran for city council . . . and won.

Having been elected Class President back in high school undoubtedly gave me the courage to try for this position, but there was also that part of me that knew I understood more about the world than my reading skills suggested. I wanted so badly to rise above the place where I was that I was willing to risk taking on a leadership task even though I couldn't read. That fire had always been inside me. I had wanted to be normal so badly—since back in first grade—that I continued to seek ways to help me feel both ordinary and successful.

I served on the council for four years and no one knew I could not read. This in itself amazed me, although I never really worried about the papers in front of us because we mostly just talked about the issues. I was and have always been a good listener, and I seem to be able to remember much more than the average person, so no one ever noticed that I was not reading the material.

Later in my life, when an article came out in the newspaper about me being dyslexic, Dr. Wayne Emerson, a local veterinarian who served on the council with me, came up to me and commented on how well I had done without being able to read. He wasn't the only one.

During my time on the council we had to deal with a lawsuit. In that process I learned so much about different kinds of people, legal terminology relative to laws and governance, as well as the need for compromise. All of these experiences gave me insight into the complexities of making change happen as well as learning to work with different personalities—skills that would become very important to me a few years down the road.

Most of the people on the council were college-educated and used a higher level of vocabulary than I was accustomed to. Being a councilman helped me improve my vocabulary as well as broaden my understanding of how to do city government. I always tried to be around people who were better educated and smarter than I was so I could challenge myself to be better.

In such ways I found opportunities to prove to myself that I had my own ways of being smart and understanding the world even though I could only read at a fifth-grade level. Somewhere in the back of my head I was challenging myself to prove that I was not stupid.

## Fulfilling My Dad's Words

My father's words had influenced me since I was a young boy. "Working people need their company to respect them and their needs," he often said, although back in his day workers didn't have vacations or days off and there was no one to support them and their rights.

While still involved in the city council, I began to attend Iowa caucuses to see what the politicians were all about—who matched my ideas and supported them. The president of the union at Hormel took note of this and selected me to be on the union's Political Action Committee. In this way I found another opportunity to grow, as well as to be involved in influencing elections in the state of Iowa. My habit of being open to whatever came my way and seeing where it took me was paying off. I felt good about the leadership I was able to give to my community and job. I wanted to be somebody who had more than just a menial job.

Again, I was comfortable taking on my new responsibilities because to represent my union I didn't have to read, all I had to do was listen and talk. Here was another opportunity for me to learn how to speak to people at all levels of government and experience, which increased my confidence in speaking in front of others. Being on the city council and representing my union at the state level also helped me understand what was going on in the world and gave me greater insight into managing my own life. Networking with others had always been a crucial part of who I was. Having a family of friends of diverse backgrounds and talents gave me a group I could call on during different situations that might occur in my life.

I didn't know how all these avenues would come together, but I felt there was a greater plan for me that I did not yet understand, so I just trusted in the journey.

Although making these commitments put me in a position that might make others aware of my lack of reading and writing skills, I was willing to take the risk. I guess I was tired of hiding behind my secrets.

At around the same time I was diagnosed with a rare lung disease, sarcardosis, so Wanda and I made a lot of visits to the Mayo Clinic in Rochestor, Minnesota. I learned a lot about the use of my health insurance, so other Hormel workers came to ask me questions. The office person in charge of insurance for the company suggested that I be on the insurance committee, and I happily agreed. This was my first opportunity to be an advocate for others. It made me feel good to help people get what they needed and deserved.

I encourage you to listen to that little voice in your head that challenges you to take on different issues in life and to act on them rather than sitting back or avoiding. These experiences will improve the quality of your life and take you places you might not have otherwise gone.

Chapter 8

# Shocked, Afraid and Uncertain

## Closure

In May of 1981, Hormel informed us that in one year they
would be closing the plant. At first I was horrified. I was 50
years old and still couldn't read. How would I support my family and send my daughter to college? I was flooded with all the
old feelings of fear, embarrassment and anxiety that I had felt
daily as a child. It was as if everything I'd accomplished since
then had been wiped out in an instant, turning me once again
into the little boy sitting in the back of the classroom.

When I went home and shared the news with Wanda she was
upset, too, but tried to comfort me. Everything would work out
down the road, she said. Then I realized the little voice inside
me was saying the same thing. I was even a little bit excited
about the many changes this would bring to my life. As I've said
before—I like to take advantage of such moments.

At the time Kelli was still a freshman in high school and
Wanda was working full time for Umthun Trucking Company,
just blocks from our house. She was so smart. When comput-
ers first came out she knew how to use them like no one else.
Everyone was always calling her for help. She was a very good

employee, finding and collecting fuel taxes that the company wasn't even aware they were owed.

I'd worked for Hormel long enough to draw a small pension and keep my health insurance, but those benefits weren't enough to support my family or help Kelli with college. Besides, I wanted to work; I was not ready to retire. But what could I do without being able to read? My usual avoidance trick of telling people "I forgot my glasses" wouldn't work; the truth was I didn't even wear glasses. And meantime I couldn't even fill out job applications properly. How could I find work that didn't involve reading?

A friend who knew I was about to be unemployed offered me the opportunity to be a crop adjustor. "All you have to do is fill out the application." I thanked him, but as I headed home I was reluctant to consider the job. For one thing, it's easy to "just fill out the application" . . . if you can read. To me, reading an application was like taking a test or, worse, trying to climb a mountain without training or equipment. And even if I somehow got the job, what then? Anyone living in a rural, agricultural area knew what a crop adjustor did—and it involved reading and filling out insurance forms.

But I needed the job so I could support my family. When I got home I talked with Wanda and together we came up with a plan.

The manager from Farmer's Mutual Hail Insurance Company called me to meet at a local restaurant for an interview. As I walked in I was nervous. *What if he asks me to read something? What if I can't answer his questions because I don't know what the papers in front of me say?*

We greeted each other and I sat down and ordered some coffee. He asked me about my hobbies and interests and I started

*Last Reader Standing*

to relax. After a few minutes of conversation he handed me the application and asked me to fill it out. I told him I wanted to think about the job, when in reality I would be taking the application home to have Wanda help me fill it out.

After I left the restaurant and looked the application over I realized I probably could have filled it out on the spot after all; I'd just been too nervous to focus. It turned out that the only things I needed to fill out were my name, address, high school and previous employer . . . all of which I had learned to spell.

Although the manager gave me two days to decide if I wanted the job, he said it was mine if I wanted it. So I took it. I actually started work even before the Hormel plant closed. Crop adjusting was a seasonal job, and I wanted to show the insurance company I was eager to get started.

But the other problem remained: I would have to fill out all the paperwork associated with crop adjusting. As I said it was an insurance matter. Farmers purchased insurance against the loss of their crops from storms, fires or other catastrophic events. My job was to visit farms where claims were being made, look at the damages, then write up and submit the claim. As a result I had to memorize how to write out many new words because I didn't know how to spell them. Every evening I diligently rewrote the day's paperwork because my handwriting was so poor and I had many misspellings to correct. Wanda patiently helped me with it all. She knew how important this was to me and never complained that we spent her evenings doing my work.

With Wanda's help I became a successful crop adjustor. The insurance company wanted me to return the following season, but meanwhile I needed to find some kind of work to fill in the remainder of the year.

One day I ran into the wife of the principal of the local elementary school. She knew the Hormel plant was closing. "What are you doing now, Archie?" she asked. When I explained my situation she told me the school district was looking for bus drivers. I told her I was interested, and she suggested I call her husband.

He called me first. "Hey Archie, I'm in desperate need of bus drivers."

"I'm not doing anything," I said. "So why not?"

The next thing I knew I was going to the Highway Patrol office to pick up study materials for the chauffer's license I needed to be a bus driver. Needless to say, having to study for this test was stressful since I couldn't actually read the materials. Wanda read them to me first, and then we read them together. After that I just kept reading them over and over. Still, thinking about taking the written test made me want to give up.

By chance, as I was preparing for my chauffer license test Kelli was studying for her driver's test. Since I was studying way more than her, I joked that I didn't think she was studying hard enough. We drove together to another town where the test was being given. She, like any teen, was excited to get her driver's license. I, on the other hand, was nervous.

Later, as we left the building, Kelli told me she got every answer right.

I sighed. "I missed passing the test by a single question. There were two questions I had right the first time and then changed."

Two days later I drove to another town and retook the test. This time I passed. Later another bus driver drove me in a school bus to the test center so I could use the bus for the driving test. I passed and drove the bus home.

But the process still wasn't over. The State of Iowa required a driver to attend special classes in order to get certified. That meant I had to go to the local community college. I'd heard that there wasn't much written work to do; mostly the class consisted of watching movies and taking a first aid test. So I took the class and studied for the test, both with Wanda and by myself. I worked as hard as I'd ever worked for anything. If I didn't pass I wouldn't be able to drive a bus, and I'd be embarrassed every time I saw the principal and his wife. They'd know I wasn't able to get this job.

In the end I felt pretty good about the material I had studied, and that little voice was busy in my head again: *Ah, just go for it, Archie. You can do it.* The voice wasn't kidding: for the first time in my life, I took a test and got every answer right! Another hurdle jumped, and now I had a job that would help me take care of my family.

I keep telling you about this little voice that's guided me since childhood. In case some of you haven't learned to listen to your own little voice, let me help you understand how to do this.

I believe this voice is my spiritual connection. Some people might call it God or a guardian angel or a spirit guide. Regardless, that voice is there to guide you, to help you make good decisions in your life. It is not evil and will not take you down a bad path. I encourage you to develop a relationship with your little voice by learning to listen to it and allowing it to lead you. Sometimes people are so busy in today's overstimulated craziness that they may have a difficult time hearing themselves . . . take time to nurture this relationship and you will begin to live the life you were intended.

# Night Work

There were nine routes for the bus drivers. All of the drivers except me were women. None of the other drivers wanted to take on the night jobs, so I was as busy as I wanted to be, driving kids to sporting events and other extracurricular activities. I was tickled that these jobs made me extra money but also let me attend the activities myself and feel like a part of the school.

My neighbor was both a high school teacher and the wrestling coach. He always wanted me to be the driver for his team because he knew he could call me any time with schedule changes. Every week the team gave a t-shirt to the outstanding player of the week. One night after I got them all home safely through a blizzard, they awarded me the shirt.

Driving a bus was less reading-intensive than my summer crop adjusting job, and gave me a break from the rigors of paperwork. While some people might think that driving all those kids around would be stressful, for me reading and writing were far greater concerns.

Chapter 9

# Exposing My Secret

## Running

In 1982, two years after I began my new careers, Wanda read me a newspaper article about Olympic Decathlon Gold Medalist Bruce Jenner. She read not only about Jenner's athletic achievements but also about his struggles with a learning disability called Dyslexia.

The more I heard about Jenner, the more I recognized my similarities to him in both athletic ability and reading problems—and the trouble those problems caused. The fulfilling life I had created despite being a non-reader was threatened every time I got reminded of my disability. It was still easy for me to find myself in that back-of-the-room desk in first grade, feeling the shame and pain I could not seem to erase.

As Wanda read on, the article described how Jenner had been tested and determined to be dyslexic. He was sharing his disability with the world because he wanted to encourage other people who might struggle with this same disability.

"Archie," Wanda said, "I think we need to find out more about this. I'm going to the library tomorrow to see if there are any books about dyslexia."

"That sounds good, Wanda," I said. Then she suggested that I look into being tested myself, and the old fears instantly returned: what if it turned out I wasn't dyslexic, but stupid? I wasn't ready to commit to anything that might have an ending like that. It was just too painful to consider exposing the things I'd been hiding from all my life.

But Wanda was a very bright woman who loved me and wanted to help. In the library she found a book titled *Reversals*, by Eileen Simpson. The author was a psychologist who shared the label of dyslexic. Ms. Simpson's experiences in life were so similar to mine that there were times, as Wanda and I read the book together, that we had to stop because we were blinded by tears. The tears were of sadness, but also of hope because someone else knew what I was experiencing. I'd worked so hard to push away the pain and failure I had faced since I was a little boy. At the same time, I was grateful for my wife and her relentless support and love of me.

So—reluctantly and still afraid of being labeled stupid—I began to look for answers. I figured schools might have a direction for me, since they tested kids, so I decided to call the local high school to talk with the counselor, Roger Williams. We knew each other from school events for which I'd driven the bus. That made calling him seem at least possible, although on the other hand I didn't want him to think less of me.

My heart was pounding out of my chest as I picked up the phone in the kitchen and considered what I'd say to him. There was no way around it: I had to tell this man I couldn't read. I had never actually said those words to *anyone*, not even Wanda. So I put the receiver back on the cradle. I'd go for a run and think this through.

I liked to run about three miles, but that day I felt like I could run a marathon. My mind raced faster than my feet so I tried to slow my thoughts down and prepare my questions.

When I returned home I was ready to make the call. I dialed the number and when the secretary answered I asked to speak to the counselor. I was hoping he'd be busy so I could just leave a message, but he picked up on the first ring.

I took a deep breath. "Hello, Roger, this is Archie Willard."

"Hello, Archie. How are you? I haven't seen you in a while."

"Well, this is kind of a long story. My wife and I read an article in the paper about Bruce Jenner being dyslexic, and . . . well, I wonder if I'm dyslexic, so I'm calling to see if the school could test me."

"Gosh, Archie, I'm sorry, but the school doesn't have any programs like that. I'm not even aware of any services in the region. I'm really sorry I can't help you."

"Well, thank you for your time . . . ."

"I'm sorry, Archie, but good luck with your search."

I plopped down at the kitchen table, awash in shame. Wanda meant well, but it was time for me to forget all this foolishness and put it all behind me. It was just too hard to feel like that kid in the back of the room again.

But the little voice in my head wouldn't stop challenging me. It knew that my real fear was that I might find out I was stupid, not dyslexic. That was the dread I'd carried with me since first grade. *Don't be afraid*, the voice said. *Just keep searching for a place to get tested.*

Although the emotional ride was taking a toll on me, after a while I decided to plug ahead anyway. I did want the answers. Wanda and I decided that I should speak with my doctor,

George Hogenson. I felt comfortable talking with him. He was very easy to talk with, and patient confidentiality made me feel safer about exposing myself. Still, as I sat in his office waiting to be seen I felt the old anxiousness return. *What will he think of me? What if he doesn't have any answers either?*

"Hi George," I said as Dr. Hogenson entered the room.

"Hi, Archie. What brings you here today?"

I explained about the Bruce Jenner article and said I thought I had the same problem. "Do you know if there's a way for me to be tested for my reading problem?"

"None of my patients have ever asked me to be tested for a reading problem," he said.

Embarrassment and shame immediately rose inside me, but Dr. Hogenson wasn't finished. "We're going to find some answers, Archie. I'll call the medical school I attended and see if they have information for us."

While I sat there silently, my heart pounding out of my chest again, he made some calls to The University of Iowa. My mind raced. *This is stupid and I'm stupid and why am I putting myself in this position?*

Finally Dr. Hogenson hung up and smiled. "The Department of Neurology has agreed to conduct the exam."

I couldn't believe it. I didn't even know what to say. When I left the exam room I wasn't sure I could focus enough to find my way to the parking lot.

## The Test

December 1983 found me waiting in the Neurology Department of the University of Iowa in Iowa City. This was it. On this day I would be tested to find out if I was dyslexic or just stupid.

I was excited, but embarrassed to have to tell more people that I couldn't read. But I had to do it—for myself and my dear Wanda. I owed it to her for all the support and love she had shown me.

I was given a physical and a whole battery of mental tests. It seemed strange that I had to go through physical tests to find out if I was dyslexic. They did a CAT scan of my brain and gave me an intelligence test, then tested my reading level. They wanted me to come back in a month to go over the results.

In January, Wanda and I drove back to the University. Neither of us had much to say. I was so anxious that it took all my mental energy just to keep the car on the road.

At the Neurology Department the doctor entered the room where I sat beside Wanda, looked me in the eye and said, "Archie, your brain is healthy and you are above average in intelligence—but you have severe dyslexia."

I didn't even know if I was breathing as he said those words. It took a moment to filter in, and then I just smiled. The labels of "stupid" and "too lazy to learn" had been replaced with "dyslexic." At last I knew why I couldn't read; all those years of not knowing were over.

I asked the doctors where I could find help to get better, but he didn't know what direction to send me. It didn't matter. I finally felt good about myself.

I'd told the doctors about my mother's reading problems, and how my grandfather signed his name with an X, and they said that dyslexia undoubtedly ran in my family. On our drive back home Wanda said, "So that explains why you always open the cereal box from the wrong end. I thought you did it just to annoy me." We laughed.

Our educational system does not want to put labels on students, but I think there are good labels as well as bad. People need to know what their problems are because dyslexia is something that never goes away. It cannot be cured. Those afflicted with dyslexia need to find ways to work around it just to survive. The best thing that ever happened to me was to be able to replace the label of "dumb" with "dyslexic." I had a learning disability, not a lack of intellect.

Ever since Wanda and I read the article about Bruce Jenner, a fire began burning inside me that lit the motivation for me to find out more.

Chapter 10

# Most People Don't Know
# I Can't Read

## My Tutor

I didn't know what to expect as I drove to my first day of tutoring. My emotions were flying all over the place. Although I was committed to doing this, it was very difficult for me to start this program. As I pulled up to the building the conversation I had with myself went like this: "I don't really have a reading problem, but maybe I need some help."

The first time I drove around the block I was bargaining with myself, trying to convince myself to park the car and go inside.

During the second turn around the block I said to myself, *The problem was the teachers I had and the materials they used; it's their fault I can't read, not mine.*

In the middle of the third circuit I finally parked and walked toward the building.

As I opened the door I wondered if they could really help me. What a long road it had been for me to reach this day and time, now I just needed the courage to find out what lay ahead.

I had signed up for tutoring because of another article Wanda had discovered, this time about a girl who couldn't read and who got help. Without Wanda I would never have found out about Bruce Jenner and dyslexia, or about getting tested, never mind looked for a way to improve my reading skills.

I had called Iowa Central Community College, where the girl in the article had received tutoring, and they told me they'd send a tutor to my town. But I declined the offer. Poor Wanda. It had to be frustrating for her to watch me struggle with accepting my disability and the help I so badly needed.

Finally, after much prodding by Wanda and Kelli, I called the college back to ask if I could come to their adult reading program instead of them coming to me. The 26 mile distance would help ensure that nobody in my small, close-knit community would find out what I was doing. The college was fine with that.

I met with Jane Hobart, the director, who introduced me to my tutor, Maxine. The moment I saw Maxine I knew she had my best interests at heart. We talked about everyday things for a while, then she said, "Archie, I'm going to try to determine your reading level so we can decide how to best help you."

My experiences as a child had taught me how to read people, and everything about Maxine told me she was a caring person I could trust.

From her evaluation Maxine established my reading level to be about that of a fifth-grader. She explained that we would read together and work on increasing my sight vocabulary. Although she understood how to help me build some basic reading skills, she admitted that she didn't know anything about dyslexia itself.

I'd compare how I felt after that first session to the way I felt after running laps. When I got home I had to take a nap. But

I also had a revelation: Things needed to be better for adults with reading problems. People like me should be able to find out what's wrong with them and get help sooner and I was going to devote the rest of my life to making that happen. I didn't know how I'd do it, but I'd find out. Wanda and I began reading books about learning disabilities to learn as much as we could.

Meanwhile my weekly sessions with Maxine continued. We read short stories about people with learning disabilities that were written for adults at my level, and solved crossword puzzles. During one session I said, "Maxine, I need confidence in my new job as a claims adjustor. I need help with writing and filling out the forms. Can we build my tutoring around that?"

"I'll do my best, Archie." So Maxine and I began to role-play. She would act as if she had a claim and then help me fill out the forms. Later, I used those as models. What a gift Maxine gave me to increase my belief in myself and to do my job well!

It turned out I was also Maxine's first student. She had formed the adult tutoring program, then retired, only to return as a volunteer. She was a tenacious teacher who also became a dear friend.

## An Expanding World

"Archie," Maxine said one day as we were finishing our session, "I'd like you to bring a sack lunch next week."

"Why?"

"Once a month the Fort Dodge Library has a guest speaker. We'll go listen to him. People who don't read lack a broad understanding of culture, and I'd like to give you some experiences to expand how you think about the world."

I thought about it for a minute. "Why not?"

Our monthly to the Fort Dodge Library proved to be very interesting and did give me knowledge I would not have gained elsewhere. If you are a New Reader you should find ways to do this for yourself. It's important for you to be aware of your strengths and use them to your advantage. Listening and remembering have always been my greatest self-development tools.

Maxine encouraged me to read books because, she said, "You build reading skills by reading, just like an athlete has to work out and practice."

I was too embarrassed to go to the library to get books appropriate for my reading level, so I began to read the Nancy Drew books Kelli had accumulated. I read all 26 of those, then went to the library and finished the series. This was not the kind of reading that builds knowledge, but it did improve my reading skills.

By then Kelli was a senior in high school, and occasionally accompanied me to my tutoring sessions. While there she helped tutor other people. I was very proud of her for doing this. Kelli had been part of my development since the day Wanda read the article about Bruce Jenner, and would remain an ally and supporter.

Later, in college, she joined a service fraternity where she influenced the other members to volunteer as tutors at the local community college in programs much like mine. She showed me what it meant to be an advocate.

After two and a half years my tutor said, "Archie, I'd like you to speak to a group of kids at Cooper Elementary School who have learning disabilities and tell them about your experience of becoming a New Reader."

At first I felt my usual resistance to going public about my reading problems, but how could I possibly say no to someone who had devoted over two years of her life to tutoring me at no charge?

Chapter 11

# My Ordinary Life Inspires Others?

## Not in the Back of the Room

It had been four years since my diagnosis of dyslexia, and 52 years since my first grade teacher stuck me in the back of the room. Now I had to face a group of people far younger than I, who at least had an opportunity to understand their disabilities. I'd thought about what I wanted to say, but the more I considered it the more confused I became. Sitting in front of those kids and watching their antics and discomfort reminded me of how I had tried to not let anyone see my pain when I was their age.

So finally I decided to just tell them about my life.

"I started off with a lot of hopes and dreams for the future," I said. "I wanted to be somebody special. When I realized I couldn't read like the rest of the kids, I lost my dreams." I shared how school had been for me, and how I eventually came to be standing there telling them my story. "I didn't really start living again until I began being open about my reading problems," I concluded. "It's important for you to be open about your disability so you won't have the monkey on your back telling you to try and hide your problem and be someone you're not."

As I finished I could see in the faces of the kids that I had given them hope—and that was how I became an advocate for literacy. From that one experience I decided I was going to dedicate my life to making a difference for others who were struggling like me. I didn't know exactly how I would do it but I knew I would find a way. Or perhaps I should say it found me. Since that first speech I've been invited to many classrooms to share my story, and I'm still amazed every time that my ordinary life inspires others to feel hopeful.

Wanda and I lived next door to a couple who were attending Iowa State University working on their Masters Degrees in Education. One day Marlis stopped over and said, "Archie, I've heard about your speeches and I wonder if you'd come to my university to talk to the graduate students about being a New Reader."

By then I'd done enough speaking that I replied without hesitation: "I'd be happy to."

Dr. Ruth Barnhart, the professor, liked my speech and her students' reaction so much that she had me return to give my talk not just once, but once every quarter for the next eight years.

Later I would encounter many of these graduate students—now teachers—at conferences on learning disabilities. By then I was seeking opportunities to keep current on the research regarding dyslexia, just as my tutor Maxine had taught me to do. I could see the full circle: me sharing with those college students who were now teaching and reconnecting with me. Many of them invited me to speak at their schools. One even invited me to participate in a wellness event that was being held for both staff and students in Ames.

By then I was also volunteering two days a week at Eagle Grove Middle School, listening and encouraging learning-disabled kids to read, so I talked with the principal about taking some of the kids to the wellness event. The principal, Mr. Woodall, knew me from growing up in the neighborhood. "Mike," I said, "I'd like the kids to attend this wellness program so they can experience something outside their school about learning disabilities. I want them to see that learning problems are bigger than them and their school, and affect many people. Do you think that's possible?"

"Archie, I'd be happy to help you give these kids the opportunity."

At the wellness workshop people spoke about a variety of disabilities. I talked about what it was like to be dyslexic. It was a great opportunity to connect with others and make a difference. By speaking about not being able to read and write well I felt I was opening the door for others to share their challenges.

A local meteorologist, Pam Dale, spoke about her disability due to an auto accident. When I finished with my talk she invited the students and me to visit her television station, WOI. It was a wonderful opportunity for the kids to see a television studio as well as a beautiful example of how to make connections. There was something about Ms. Dale that really reached out to people—a valuable experience for the students to witness.

One time as I was getting ready to share my story at a school the Special Education teachers warned me not to be surprised if the kids were restless and noisy. Some of the kids had trouble focusing and settling down, they said. "Don't take it personally, they're like that with everyone."

But after I started speaking there wasn't another sound in the room. I think it was because the kids had never heard an adult who was struggling like them talking openly about the challenges we shared. Later the teachers gave the kids the opportunity to ask questions. They were not shy and asked the same questions over and over in different ways to make sure they really understood. "Do you like to read now?" "Do you still have trouble reading?"

"I don't like to read long books," I replied.

They also wanted to know if the other members of my family could read well or if I was the only one who couldn't read. I told them about my mother and grandfather because I knew that might help some of them.

This wasn't a one-time experience for me. Time and again the audiences I spoke to had a similar reaction.

One event led to another. There were engagements at schools within a hundred-mile radius of my hometown, and then events at universities and conferences, prisons and churches from one end of the United States to the other, and finally speaking trips to Eastern Europe. Who would have ever guessed that all that would happen because I lost my job and had to confront my fears and secrets?

## Fighting for Freedom

There is nothing better than to feel you are free. Martin Luther King said this in his famous speech, "Free at last, free at last . . ." But there are many people who are not free for many different reasons. Growing up without being able to read robs children of many opportunities; bad memories of school can make them lose hope and become frustrated enough to give up on their dreams.

If you don't have hope it is like running a race with no finish line. I think Martin Luther King would be eager to share his words with New Readers—those whose struggles with their challenges can keep them from having the lives they dream of. The quality of my life kept improving as my self-esteem and confidence grew—no more hiding, no more pretending. Plus I found a whole new world of learning and information available that I had never been able to access before.

Learning to read was changing my life.

Part Three

# Becoming an Advocate

*If you don't have hope it's hard to know what direction
you are going and it is impossible to follow your dreams.*
*—Archie Willard*

Chapter 12

# Where Are the Dyslexic People?

## My First Conference

At one of my tutoring sessions Maxine said, "Archie, I think we're about done. I've taken you as far as we can go together. I know you're looking for more answers about dyslexia, so here's a flyer I received in the mail that might help you find some answers. I think you should go to this conference in Cedar Rapids."

My tutoring with Maxine was ending? I felt afraid. I wasn't ready to fly on my own without the support of Maxine.

According to the brochure, the conference was being hosted by the Iowa State branch of the Orton Dyslexia Society. Dr. Orton was one of the early researchers into learning disabilities and dyslexia. As early as the 1930's he had noticed that a lot of the boys who struggled with learning were also left-handed. He began to research this relationship further at the University of Iowa. After his death in 1949 the society was formed and named in his honor.

Known today as the International Dyslexia Association, the organization boasts more than forty branches worldwide and continues to function as a non-profit organization advocating for and educating on issues related to dyslexia.

I drove the 150 miles to Cedar Rapids and arrived at the conference site ahead of time. Then I sat in the hotel lobby thinking, *Should I go in or not?* I kept watching people entering the room where the conference was being held to see if I could spot another dyslexic person, whatever that meant. I still really didn't know.

Finally I decided I'd better just stop trying to figure it out and get in there. My little voice was at it again: *Just do it.*

When I walked in I discovered that pretty much everyone else there was a doctor, psychologist or special education teacher.

"Where are the dyslexic people?" I asked at the registration desk.

"Really," they said, "you're the only one—well, except Dr. Paul Beard, who's also a veterinarian."

I thought, *Wow, another dyslexic—who managed to become a veterinarian.* Still, I was disappointed. I'd hoped to meet other people with similar problems so I could find out how they felt and dealt with dyslexia in their lives.

"Maybe I don't belong here," I said.

The registration people told me they were glad to have Dr. Beard and me in attendance because we could add credibility to what was being presented. And I was certainly glad to meet Paul, who had accomplished something I couldn't despite his own dyslexia. I think we bonded because we understood each other's daily challenges. It didn't seem to matter to either of us that our life paths had been different; we were grateful to know another person who understood what it was like to be dyslexic. Paul and I stayed in touch and became great friends and mutual supporters.

Now that my problem had a name I wanted to learn everything I could about it, but the conference provided only half the education I required. The experts provided information to help me improve myself, but I also wanted to learn from others who were personally living with dyslexia. Unfortunately it turned out that not very many dyslexics attend conferences.

*Where can I meet other learning-disabled people as well as learn more about my problem?* I wondered. It seemed that what I was looking for just didn't exist.

When the Orton Society invited me to join their state membership I decided to give it a try, and eventually became a member of the Board. Although I often asked questions to which they had no answers, they kept me around because I was dyslexic. Later I started attending their national meetings as well.

The national meetings gave me an opportunity to hear big, high powered speakers—but they often talked over my head and I had to ask other specialists what the words meant. Even then I still had questions, and felt more and more certain that I needed other learning-disabled people to help me find answers.

I suggested getting more learning disabled people involved with the Orton Society so they could learn about their condition and how to deal with the challenges in their lives, but the organization wanted to focus on research and development. I was making waves and people were getting to know me. The state Board members thought the national program might have more avenues for me, so they nominated me to be on the Board of the national organization.

When I received a letter from the National Orton Society telling me there wasn't room on the Board for anyone with my qualifications, I ended my participation with this organization. As fine a group as it was, it was the wrong avenue for me to get more learning disabled people involved.

Chapter 13

# How Can I Make Things Better
# For People Like Me?

## Making More Waves

After hearing me speak at an Orton meeting, a woman from the
Learning Disabilities Association of America contacted me to
be on their Board. While the objectives of the two organizations
were similar, the Learning Disabilities Association seemed more
tolerant of having learning disabled people participate.

In 1990, I was given the opportunity to speak at their national
conference. These organizations didn't really know what to do
with me. They liked that I was a dyslexic person who was looking for answers, but the other Board members were, again, all
professionals in the educational or medical fields. I felt like I
was being used more as a figurehead than anything, and not
really listened to by the members. Nothing against the organizations, the membership or their work; I just didn't fit in.

I wanted learning disabled people who were struggling with
their problem to have a voice. I wanted them to receive the
encouragement they needed to continue growing and to help
themselves. I'd met many professionals who were striving to
educate, but they weren't always willing to listen to the people

actually living with dyslexia. Even those who *were* willing to listen had already invested so much money and time in ongoing projects that they didn't want to change direction.

I had a different mission in mind, and worked hard to convince the National Board to allow me to speak at the National Disabilities Conference in Chicago. They finally and reluctantly agreed to give me a small group session.

## Functional

I delivered my speech about living with dyslexia to a group of only about twelve people, all professionals. They didn't respond much. Later, thinking it over, I decided the audience had been afraid that asking me questions might embarrass me. Or maybe they just didn't know what to ask me. At any rate it was a good experience for me and hopefully each of the attendees took something that I said home with them.

The only audience member who spoke with me afterwards was Dr. Ann Schafer, representing a California learning organization. She congratulated me on my courage to speak out and encouraged me to continue.

Later, I received a letter from Dr. Schafer encouraging me to apply to be a speaker at a national conference in Minnesota. There I gave a similar speech to a similar audience. I also met John Corcoran, a now-famous dyslexic and the author of *The Teacher Who Couldn't Read*. Ann had been his tutor, and he was also attending and speaking at the conference.

"I'm a university graduate," John said, "with a Bachelor's Degree in Education and Business Administration and over 90 additional graduate units. I've attended school for 35 years, half of them as a professional educator. In acquiring these experiences, I could not read a textbook or write the answer to an essay question. This is the first public acknowledgment that I have ever made that I have been a functional illiterate for almost 50 years."

## The Third Dimension

The more conferences I attended the harder I tried to convince professionals to listen to dyslexics about what it was like to live with dyslexia. It was tough going. Although many of the professionals had methods for diagnosis and techniques for remediation, trying to understand the dyslexic person seemed to be missing from the formula.

Still, despite the frustrations I was learning a great deal about the academic, research side of learning disabilities. At one conference I found out about "the third dimension," a twist that learning-disabled people have in their learning style. I recognized it as what I used when I did public speaking and the other activities I was getting involved in.

The third dimension refers to a way of communicating without using black and white or yes and no answers. For example, when I prepared for a speech I didn't write anything down, I simply recalled the stories I wanted to use and remembered the beginning and ending of those stories. I filed this like a folder in a cabinet in my brain, and then I was prepared for my speech.

So while the academics weren't able to give me what I was looking for in terms of involving more dyslexics in research and outreach, at least the knowledge I gained enabled me to better explain things to the groups I came in contact with.

## Giving New Readers A Voice

In 1990, Miriam Temple, then the Director of Adult Education at the Iowa Department of Public Education, invited program directors from the fifteen state community colleges to bring New Readers to their first reading congress. Entitled "Literacy in the Home and Workplace, 1990," it used as its model the National Program of New Readers.

A man named Steve and I, both New Readers in the same tutoring program, were invited by Jane Hobart, the tutoring program director, to attend the State of Iowa literacy meetings to share our stories. We also had a part in planning the conference. I was very excited. For the first time I was going to hear other dyslexic people talk about what they were doing and how they survived with their challenges. Because of my recent speaking experience I was given the job of being a moderator, to talk about the workplace.

Initially, each dyslexic was asked to get up and explain who he or she was and where they were from. Most of these people had never attended a conference or spoken out loud about being a New Reader before, and I saw their pain and discomfort regarding all they had experienced.

But once the small groups started and the New Readers became more comfortable talking, you couldn't shut them up. They were comfortable, excited and ready to share their stories. I was happy to see the joy in their faces. By sitting in round table and listening to each other's stories they were actually teaching each other how to make adjustments and modifications in their lives. It was at this point that many of the New Readers asked me how they could speak to groups like I was doing. This was exactly what I'd been looking for, a way for New Readers to advocate for themselves and others.

This was my first opportunity to see so many New Readers together. There were approximately 90 attendees and I was excited and somewhat surprised to see such a variety of people. Some were just out of high school and others were older than me—and I was sixty. As a result of their moderator-led groups the attendees created a list of the challenges New Readers typically deal with, and these proclamations were given to the Governor of Iowa. It was a token gesture, but monumental in that the New Readers now felt listened to and respected.

When I returned home and reflected on what had occurred at this congress I realized that this was the avenue I had been seeking. I wanted to call Miriam Temple and ask her to continue the round table meetings . . . but who was I? Just a New Reader. She was the State Director for Iowa. Did I really have the right to call and ask something of a woman like her?

*Just do it*, said the little voice.

After I got my courage up, I called Ms. Temple and said, "I thought this conference was very successful. Are you going to have another one?"

She told me no, it was just a one-time thing. But I didn't let up. I stressed how much the conference had helped all the attendees, hitting the point again and again until she finally said she'd host another such conference,if I promised I'd have several people from the round table groups commit to speaking at it. I agreed.

Everyone I spoke to was terrified by the request but, in the end, agreed to assume the responsibility.

Looking back, I see that this arena for dyslexic people was exactly the forum I'd been pushing for. All I had to do next was figure out how to keep it going.

Chapter 14

# Stepping Into a
# Professional Role

## Building Relationships

Jane Hobart, the Coordinator of the Iowa Community College Literacy program, invited me to become an Adult Literacy
Recruiter, taking one of five positions. I turned her down. I
didn't think I was capable.

The following year Jane asked again. This time she said,
"Archie, after all your traveling to conferences in the last few
years, speaking to thousands of people and advocating for other
New Readers, you can do this."

I thought, *She's right. If I can do crop adjusting I can do this.*
"Okay Jane," I said, "I'll give it a try. But I'll need some extra
help and understanding when I make mistakes."

"I'll be happy to help you."

That's how in the fall of 1991 I became the Adult Literacy
coordinator for two counties in Iowa.

At this point I understood that dyslexia cannot be cured. I
could work to find my way around the obstacles to find a better
life, but I had to accept that my dyslexia could not be fixed. To

move ahead I would always have to find different strategies and let people know what I needed.

As a recruiter I had to work with the other recruiters, build relationships with New Readers, find tutors and encourage them to learn to advocate for themselves. I also continued my own speaking engagements. These were all the things I valued, and the other four recruiters were so accepting and encouraging that my job became very enjoyable. Often the talks I gave let me connect with potential New Readers and tutors, so I was doing both things at the same time.

In December one of the recruiters had her nephew drive us in his limousine to our Christmas party. As it happened, all the other recruiters except me were women. As we crawled out of the limo a bystander called to me, "Wow, how do you rate having a limo with all those ladies?"

"This is my harem," I replied.

## Teacher, Recruiter . . . Teacher

One of the speaking engagements I valued most was being invited to speak at GED graduation ceremonies at the prisons. Generally, there was a social after my speech where the prisoners could come up and talk with me one on one. Most of the time they wanted to tell me that they could not read either. On one occasion a prisoner who was going to be released three days before the graduation ceremony actually asked to stay behind bars long enough to go through the ceremony. I was very moved by this.

My favorite part of being a recruiter was when I met people who were struggling to read and shared how I'd gone through the same things they were going through. Some of the other recruiters were not New Readers and had trouble getting students to go to the tutoring program, so they'd ask me to intervene. I had better success because non-readers felt comfortable with me, someone who knew how they felt.

Another thing I enjoyed about this job was that the college used me for public relations, to explain our program to service groups in the community. I loved doing this.

Yet another opportunity blossomed when one of the community colleges asked me to teach an adult education class entitled *Understanding Learning Disabilities*. Yes, me—a guy who had struggled with school all his life—was going to teach a college class. I used the videotape by Rick Lavoie, "How Difficult Can This Be? The F.A.T. City Workshop," which showed more than words can explain what it is like to be dyslexic.

During the class I said to the audience, "If I tell you something you'll forget it, but if I show you something you'll remember it . . . and if I *involve* you'll understand it." I demonstrated this by inviting the audience to be the parts of a dyslexic brain. One person represented the front, left part of the brain where reading and processing takes place. Another person was the back of the brain where the signals are sent for what you see. I placed two more people on the sides to represent what you hear and one person in the middle to be the receptor for what we touch.

Finally, I assigned other people to stand where they would function as blocks to the signal areas. This showed how the brain has to re-route signals, which causes a time lag. I wanted the students to understand that dyslexia, a learning disability, is a processing problem that has nothing to do with intelligence.

The class was so well received by educators and parents that the four other community colleges invited me to do the same. It was during these classes that I began to realize how important it was for parents whose children have learning disabilities to be advocates for their offspring. Parents in the audience were so excited that they wanted me to attend their children's IEP (Individual Educational Plan) meetings at their schools.

In doing this I learned the importance of parents understanding the process their school districts used for testing and placement. Also, there are state and federal laws parents need to be aware of so they know exactly what their child is entitled to. Finally, I encouraged parents to learn how to ask respectfully for what they do not understand as they learned to be their child's advocate.

I encouraged the parents of young children to keep a positive attitude towards their child's challenges while seeking to understand the problems they would face and develop coping skills. Parents also need to model the behaviors that they want their child to eventually do for themselves. I found out that most colleges will accept an IEP, so it's important to have a current Plan ready as a teen leaves high school. This will allow the student to receive tutoring services while they attend college.

Parents of learning-disabled children often told me that they were not happy with the testing the school did and asked me to recommend a better testing site. I sent them to the Reading Center in Rochester, Minnesota to see Jean Osmond. I'd come to know Jean from my meetings with the Orton Society. She was a caring person, easy to work with, and parents always reported that this was a successful link for them. If you're a parent in a similar situation you might have to find a private source, such as the Reading Center, to guide you.

## Full-time Advocacy

In 1992, I decided it was time to retire from bus driving and focus on being a recruiter and speaker. Both these jobs were giving me the opportunity to advocate for literacy, but more importantly, to work on behalf of people like myself who didn't know how to find their way. I had been fortunate to have Wanda and Kelli to encourage and support me; now I was giving the same boost to others who couldn't read.

By this time I was considered a professional. Miriam Temple, Director of the Iowa Department of Education, invited me to be part of the Summer Seminar discussions that were focused on social justice. Discussions such as this were teaching me to be a critical thinker. Here was a wonderful opportunity for me to communicate with and learn from college presidents and professionals from a variety of other careers.

Chapter 15

# I Am No Longer
# Willing to Sit Back

## Settle Down

The members of the New Readers of Iowa were worried about whether their New Reader conventions would continue. We had all grown so much as a result of meeting and learning together and didn't want the opportunity to end. Miriam Temple, the Director for the Iowa Department of Adult Education, had been keeping our conferences going each year, but she would retire in December of 1998. The New Readers wrote letters to the Department Bureau Chief regarding our desire to keep the congresses going, but did not receive any replies.

In my zest to speak for the New Readers I called the Department of Education to find out who would replace Miriam. I got Miriam's boss on the phone, and she snapped, "Who put you up to this?"

I was stunned. "People with reading problems will be involved with this person, so they need to have a voice in deciding who that will be."

"There's a process in place, and you don't need to be concerned with that decision."

91

"Well, I feel that the New Readers have a right to be a part of it," I said just before she hung up.

I called the Bureau Chief, Dr. Janice Ferdell. When her secretary asked me what I wanted, I said, "I want the New Readers to have a voice in the selection of the Director of Adult Education." The secretary set up an appointment for me to meet with Dr. Ferdell. Not long after that my boss at the community college where I was working as a recruiter received a call to tell me to "settle down."

That was when my tenaciousness kicked in. I was not willing to sit back and do a "wait and see." Before the beginning of the next summer seminar meeting, I told a few members about my phone call. Conrad De Jardin, a retired vice-president of Iowa Valley Community College, was there, so I asked him to go with me for moral support to my meeting with the Bureau Chief. Conrad and I had met previously and had a good working relationship.

"Yes, Archie," he said, "I'd be glad to go. I think your idea is sound and I support what you're trying to do."

I was thrilled. His presence would add weight to the meeting. I didn't want that office to later claim that they'd explained everything to me but, as a New Reader, I simply didn't understand.

I'd never been involved in a meeting like that before and wanted to conduct myself in a suitable manner. As a result I was nervous but determined to be heard. Conrad and I walked into the building together. Everyone was very civil as we shook hands and greeted each other. Dr. Ferdell and Miriam's boss were both present and both seemed a little surprised by Conrad's appearance with me.

When we sat down Dr. Ferdell asked me how she could help.

"The New Readers of Iowa have a very good track record in taking New Readers to the next step of leadership," I said. I was pretty fired up and speaking quite loudly. "So I would like us to be involved in selecting the new director. I'd also like a commitment that the state will continue to support the New Reader Conferences."

"Well, Archie," Dr. Ferdell said, "I appreciate your concerns and I respect what the New Readers have done. I thank you for coming here today."

A cordial response, but it gave no indication of if the Department would continue to financially support the conferences, never mind include New Readers in the selection process for the director position. Basically she didn't answer me at all.

Eventually we learned that the state of Iowa decided to continue their support of the New Readers conferences. They had already selected someone for the director position before I even attended that meeting, but someone in the Department of Education told me that if not for that meeting the state would have simply dropped our activities from their budget.

As a result of all this, to date the New Readers of Iowa have held 23 consecutive annual conferences. This is a claim no other state can make. And it all began in 1990 when Ms. Temple and I held the first conference, which led to forming the New Readers of Iowa.

By that time I was no longer just looking for information about learning disabilities, I was trying to be a voice, a leader, for New Readers. This was the beginning of my leading New Readers to advocate for themselves. Today we raise our own funds and the college provides a room for our conferences. The

New Readers continue to volunteer in schools as well as col-laborate with state officials to create the annual conference for New Readers. All the work is done by the New Readers, as volunteers.

## A National View of Illiteracy

"Archie," Miriam said, "I know you've been wanting to attend the National Literacy Congress in September. Well, there's an opening. If you still want to attend we'll send you as a repre-sentative."

I knew what she meant about "an opening." The New Read-ers who had previously attended the meetings of the National Congress had not followed through with leadership when they returned; Miriam had higher expectations of me.

"Thank you so much," I said. "I promise I'll use this oppor-tunity well."

When I told Wanda she said, "Archie, this is a wonderful chance for you. I'd like to go with you; then I can see Kelli, too." Kelli had been working in Washington as an aide to Rep-resentative Nagle since graduating from the University of Iowa in 1990 with a degree in International Studies.

"Of course you should come with me!" I said. "We can make a vacation out of it and enjoy some time with Kelli. It'll be great fun and hopefully enlightening as well."

The New Readers of Iowa is a state organization that evolved from the federal program of the National Literacy Congress. I'd long wanted to attend the National Literacy Congress to find out what was happening at the national level and to meet more people with learning problems. This conference had all the states involved and would give me an opportunity to work on the vision I had in the back of my head of a national organization of New Readers.

The National Literacy Congress is sponsored by Laubach Literacy and Literacy Volunteers of America. Its purpose is to bring awareness to government entities and to encourage understanding of literacy issues in the general population. The three-day schedule of the congress included speakers and many opportunities for New Readers to connect. We ate meals together as well as gathering socially in the evenings. This gave me the opportunity to store up connections for the future.

We were assigned to four different groups that attended sessions together. The sessions taught us how to talk to the press, how to use Congressional resources, how to lobby for our causes, and many other leadership skills. Although I already had my own ideas about these things, to have someone lay them out step by step was very helpful.

At the conclusion we were asked to write a proclamation about how to improve literacy in the United States, and each group picked two of its members to be their speakers. Congressmen from each state were invited to attend this final event. I had two Iowa representatives present—the best representation of any state. I felt proud that they'd taken the time to be there; it showed they had an interest in adult literacy.

I was excited when I met people from Illinois who had also formed a state New Reader group. As I was explaining my vision of a national New Reader group to Dale Christianson, the Illinois leader, he said, "Archie, I have the same dream."

We started to talk with another attendee, a woman named Pat Blackwell, from Indiana. She agreed with our thoughts about a national organization and said, "I'd love to have the

New Readers from Indiana join in this effort." I was thrilled. These people were like me—ordinary people who happened to be New Readers, and eager to provide leadership for other New Readers in their states.

Long after the congress ended, Dale, Pat and I started meeting back and forth with larger groups of people in Illinois and Iowa. We talked up the potential for our dream of a national organization comprised of New Readers from every state.

Little did I realize that I was laying the groundwork for a national organization for which I would become not only the co-founder but the president.

## My Biggest Speech Yet

The speech during which I shared the stage with Barbara occurred at this time. It was a magical event for me and one that still tops my list of the most important things I have ever accomplished. It gave me the courage to continue my journey of making a difference for New Readers, and made me aware of the importance of raising public awareness and finding ways to advance causes for literacy.

During her husband's Presidency, Barbara Bush made literacy important. The timing was perfect for what I was trying to accomplish in my own fight.

It was time for me to take the next step.

## First Speaking Engagements Outside Iowa

Jane Hobart, my Adult Literacy Program Director, handed me a conference form for the State of Illinois Literacy program. "Archie, I know you've been looking for other speaking opportunities, so why don't you to apply to be a speaker at this conference?"

I called to inquire about applying, and the person on the line said, "We'll get back to you."

Not long afterward Connie Miller from the Illinois Literacy program called. "Hello, Archie, we'd like to put you on the program as a speaker."

I was delighted—until five days later when Connie called me back. "I'm sorry, Archie, we won't be needing you after all. We have sufficient speakers at this time."

My joy turned to anger. "You led me on and got me all excited about being able to speak at your conference," I said in a loud voice, "and now you tell me I'm *not* speaking? I don't think you've been fair to me."

"Ok, Archie," she said, "I'll check it out again and get back to you." I suspect she didn't think a New Reader would speak up the way I did. In any event, she called later and told me I'd been accepted as a speaker for the conference. Interestingly, after this challenging beginning Connie and I became great friends. I think the problem was that the program planners were afraid I might not be able to speak well enough to represent my interests, and therefore hesitated on their decision. During a previous conference they had evidently had a New Reader speak who was not ready for the task.

When I entered the conference room assigned to me it turned out to be far too small for all the people waiting to hear my speech. Dale Christianson, who was going to introduce me, decided to take all 300 of us to a cafeteria where there was enough seating for everyone. I was shocked and pleased. Having so many waiting to hear me meant people had questions and wanted answers.

I spoke about my life, just as you have been reading, but

limited myself to an hour. My goal was to explain who New Readers were and what we could become if given the chance. My audience consisted mostly of professionals who headed up the literacy programs in Illinois, along with a handful of New Readers who were invited because they were receiving an award. Many people stayed afterward to ask questions.

At the end, Dale brought all the New Readers together so we could continue to talk. Some of the others came up and hugged me; some were crying and thanked me for sharing "their" story. As we took turns telling our stories we laughed and cried together. All our accounts were so similar that the other New Readers could relate and feel good that someone had the courage to get up and share their plight. I spoke many times in Illinois after that.

A couple weeks after the conference Connie told me what a good job I'd done. "Your speech was a highlight of the conference."

I was anxious to listen to every word she said, but Wanda was waiting for me to drive her to an appointment, "C'mon, Archie, I'm going to be late."

In the car I looked at her and said, "You think I'm going to hang up on somebody who's telling me how good I'm doing?" We had a good chuckle over that.

In 2000, I was invited to Northwest Missouri State in St. Joe, Missouri, to speak at a literacy weekend. When I arrived I was told that a local radio station wanted me to be on a talk show. *I can't do that!*, I thought. But then I realized I had come all this way to make a difference and I wasn't going to let my fears limit me.

It turned out to be the most fun I'd ever had in a public speaking event. It felt like it only lasted 15 minutes, but I answered questions from callers for an hour and a half. When it was over I wished I could do it again—and all I'd done was answer from my life experiences.

My speaking career has taken me so many places, from college reading programs to prisons to teaching a class about dyslexia—but always it's been about giving hope to others. To make a difference in life we must all step over our fears.

## Chapter 16

# What About Literacy In Russia?

## Crossing New Boundaries

In 1993, I received a mailing inviting me to participate in a trip to Russian as a professional in the literacy field. I thought they'd made a mistake, so I called the number on the application and explained that "I'm a dyslexic, not a professional."

"You need to talk to Dr. Joan Stoner," said the person on the phone. "She's leading the trip."

When they put me through to Dr. Stoner I repeated that I was dyslexic and she said, "I want you to be a part of this group because we need a person with a learning disability. I feel that you'll round out this delegation and help us understand through your experience."

"Well, I didn't think I qualified before," I said, "but now I'm committed to going. I look forward to meeting you in May." I've loved to travel ever since my youthful jaunts to Mexico, so I was very excited about taking a trip to Russia. I didn't feel that the United States had all the answers to literacy issues, and wanted to broaden my base of experiences and get acquainted with professionals from different areas of literacy, including other countries.

Everything was scheduled out for us: meals, rooms and sites to visit. One of the first places we went was the University of Moscow, where a professor talked about how Russia dealt with learning disabilities. I got so tired of sitting that I decided to stand, and when the professor finished her speech she came over and talked with me.

She asked if I was a Christian. I didn't expect such a personal question, but she said that since I was from the United States she knew she could ask. She said that in her country, which had been communist until two years previously, you didn't have as many choices, but she implied that there was more Christianity in Russia than one might think.

A man Wanda worked with had heard that I was going to Russia and donated a Bible, written in Russian, for me to present to someone. I still wasn't sure how to give it away when I mentioned my dilemma to another man who was part of our delegation.

"Archie," he said, "I'm from New York. I'll solve your problem." He waved his hand at a Russian citizen passing by on the street, motioning for her to come over to us.

I was embarrassed, but said, "I have this Bible that I would like to give someone." She undoubtedly didn't understand a word, but she didn't need to; her face said it all as she gladly took the Bible from me.

We'd been told that on our last day in Russia one of us would have the opportunity to speak. Our group decided it should be me because I was the only dyslexic person there. As a result I spoke to fifty faculty members at the Hertzen Institute for Pedagogical Studies in St. Petersburg, Russia, through an interpreter, as well as to the thirty people from our delegation. This was a big deal and I was very proud, considering that it was something I couldn't have even imagined doing earlier in my life.

I shared my life story, just as I had in my first speech back in 1987 with those little grade-school kids. I talked for about twenty minutes and had the feeling it went well. The faces of the audience showed appreciation, which was as much reaction as I could expect from this culture.

I was very impressed with the Russian schools. I especially liked how they tested every student before they entered school, which allowed the teachers to know from day one what potential problems a kid might have or be expected to have. This testing and measurement of skills continued throughout high school and beyond. That way kids could determine if they would go on to high level courses or to some other level of training. The plan seemed to be to assign kids to where they needed to be.

In 1995, I was able to return to Russia. Prior to leaving I went in to see my dentist for a checkup, and she said, "Archie, people in Russia have a difficult time accessing dental care. Let me send some things with you." So she gave me a hundred toothbrushes and tubes of toothpaste as gifts to hand out. The smiles I received as I distributed the dental supplies was all the thanks I needed. The hundred pieces were gone in no time at all.

Chapter 17

# Finding My Way
# In The Big Scene

## The Fellowship

One day in 1995 while I was still working as a crop adjustor, I happened to come home early to a ringing phone. I picked it up and the voice on the other end wanted to interview me about becoming one of 25 adults with reading difficulties to come to the National Institute for Literacy (NIFL) in Washington, D.C., to talk with adult learners about literacy leadership in our country.

As I hung up I wasn't sure if I said "Yay!" to myself or out loud. *I've done enough that people know I am out here fighting for literacy.* The NIFL must have become aware of me because of the National Congress I'd attended as well as other public speaking I'd done. Regardless, the NIFL meeting would be an important one for me because there I would get acquainted with other adult learners or New Readers who were also leaders in different states.

Kelli, who was now working as a lobbyist for Vietnam veterans, picked me up at the D.C. airport and we did a little sightseeing. When she dropped me off at my hotel I walked through the lobby and began to see faces I recognized from the National Congress I attended two years earlier. There was a get-together being hosted for the attendees, and as I walked in the room I felt the buzz of energy. Everyone was excited to be there and curious about what brought the others there.

"Out meetings" took place in the offices of the NIFL in downtown D.C. There were discussions about adult literacy and other topics by different speakers. NIFL wanted us to understand its purpose and functions but also to find out what capabilities adult learners have for leadership. For most of the employees and members of the Board, adult literacy was known only on paper and not through real people. One of the speakers talked about and encouraged us to apply for a fellowship with the National Institute for Literacy. I didn't really understand what she was talking about so I just put the idea away with the rest of my handouts and forgot about it.

Since Kelli was still living in D.C. I extended my trip a few days to spend time with her. As she was going through my hand-outs from meetings she saw the fellowship application and said, "Dad, you *are* going to apply for this fellowship."

"No," I said. But after we discussed what the fellowship actually meant we sat down and she helped me fill out the application. It was quite involved, requiring letters of recommendation as well as my having to write what I would like to accomplish if I were to earn the fellowship.

It turned out that it was one of the first "adult learners" fellowships ever awarded. Later that fall while I was on my second Russian trip the Institute called and left a message. When I didn't respond they called again and Wanda, concerned that they would think I wasn't interested, called them back. She informed them that I was in Russia but would be happy to accept the offer.

When I got back Wanda said, "Archie, I have some good news for you. The NIFL called and they've awarded you the fellowship."

"Wow!" I said. "It's been so long since I filled out the paper-work I just figured it wasn't going to happen."

This was going to be a life-changing event. Since it mean I'd be flying to D.C. at least once a month I made the decision to retire from my crop adjusting job. Now I could commit myself exclusively to the tasks involved in the fellowship.

On the application I had written that my goal, if I was selected, would be to "work on educating the nation about learning disabilities." When the Institute told me I was one of the six applicants accepted they asked if I'd be willing to change my focus to collecting information about the ways adult learners are involved in literacy programs. I replied, "I'm so happy to be part of this fellowship, of course I'm willing to change my focus."

In January of 1996, I traveled to Washington D.C., to meet the fellowship team. Two federal officials defined the fellowship to us. Our team consisted of two people with Ph.D.'s and two with Masters degrees all working in literacy fields, an English as a Second Language New Reader and me, a New Reader. Over-all, our goal was to develop leaders in literacy projects with the federal government providing the funds and direction.

As a Fellow my role was to collect information from literacy programs to see how they were involving New Readers. I would check on programs east of the Mississippi, while Santali, the English as a Second Language New Reader, would do the same west of the Mississippi. I set up appointments using information from surveys that had been returned by literacy programs seeking information about resources from the National Institute for Literacy.

This was a great learning experience that opened many doors for me. I got to work with and learn from the other Fellows as well as the different literacy programs I contacted. A major discovery for me in my travels was that on a nationwide basis there was very little leadership opportunity for New Readers. Without leadership, the potential for growth in literacy was limited. New Readers need to be involved because we are the only ones who truly understand what we need and it is important for each of us to be involved in creating our own solutions.

## Chapter 18

# Everything I Have Worked For

## Voice of Adult Literacy United for Education (VALUE)

Ever since my first tutoring session, I'd known that I wanted to do something to improve conditions for people with literacy problems, but wasn't sure what or how. Only as I attended conferences and got involved in literacy issues did I began to realize that the main problem was that people with literacy problems had no voice. I vowed to change that.

The first time I met Dale Christianson, a New Reader from Illinois, we began to discuss this dilemma and the seeds of thought began to grow about forming a nationwide program that would provide a voice and leadership for literacy. I began to envision what I wanted to do and shared it with everyone I came in contact with. All this was just talk until David Rosen, who did a fellowship with me in 1996, began to encourage me to follow through on my vision. He also suggested where this needed to take place.

In 1996, during one of my last meetings with the National Institute for Literacy, I was explaining my vision when one of the program people encouraged me to go for it. "When you're ready, write and request a grant. I'll punch you in the nose if you don't do it," she warned. "It's a great idea."

I got the courage to write the proposal by actively writing on a literacy discussion group website. I knew how to use the computer and benefitted from spellcheck. I knew the Institute would accept the proposal because they had encouraged me to write it and probably wouldn't expect it to be as well-written as something from a more literate person. Wanda helped me and in the end I was happy with how good it looked, so I sent it off.

Wanda and I decided to visit Kelli and see the blossoming cherry trees in Washington D.C. As long as I was there I figured I might as well stop in to see the people at the National Institute for Literacy office. They invited me to attend the budget meeting where they were going to present my request for a grant. The timing was perfect, although I was worried that I might be getting in over my head by trying to create a nationwide organization.

I felt much better when Susan Green, one of the office staff members, said, "You're basically a shoo-in to get one of the grants, Archie. Don't worry about it—but you really do need to be here tomorrow."

Although Kelli, Wanda and I had plans for the next day, they were so excited for me that they willingly went their separate way while I headed back to the Literacy office. It was worth it: the National Institute for Literacy awarded me a tax-exempt grant to create a national organization. I immediately wanted to call the people who'd take part in helping me make this happen—but I was afraid they wouldn't believe me. Finally I called five former students about forming our vision of a nationwide student organization, and to my surprise they were excited and ready for the challenge.

After that I was ready to forge ahead. These were not easy grants to get and I was very appreciative. We even received additional funds from another organization via an anonymous donor.

I have had so many wonderful experiences working with various organizations in my pursuit of knowledge, but the group that really stood out was the six of us adult learners from five different states who came together to form the student group we called VALUE: Voice of Adult Literacy United for Education. Some of us had been talking about forming such a group for years. We wanted to reach more New Readers to liberate them from their pasts and give purpose and meaning to their lives.

The six of us developed the criteria for our big meeting by coming up with a mission statement and bylaws. These were the original six members that planned VALUE: 1) Dale Christianson, from Illinois; 2) Pat Blackwell, from Indiana; 3) Archie Willard, from Iowa; 4) Ed Castor, also from Indiana; 5) Toni Cordell, from New York; and 6) John Zickefoose, from California.

Now we had a team and a name for our organization, and things just kept building from there. A lot of people gave their time, knowledge and resources. We used many professionals to advise us in planning the framework of VALUE. But the groundwork was done by the six of us New Readers. We used the internet via Listserv to invite programs to send representatives to our first national meeting of New Readers.

As David Rosen had suggested, we made the decision to host the first meeting at the Highlander, a mountain retreat in Tennessee, with a very historical past. The Highlander only allowed meetings to take place that were associated with social justice.

We made contact with the State Director of New Hampshire, who was also on the Highlander board, to rent the facility. He took our proposal to the board and they accepted our request. Deep in my mind I didn't see how they could turn us down, but I was still relieved that we had this place for the important first meeting of our national voice for literacy

Miles Horton, "the father of the Civil Rights movement," was the founder of the Highlander Folk School as well as a teacher who influenced Rosa Parks in making her decision to "stay on the bus." This was a place where different social movements had started, and it seemed appropriate that a social movement for literacy should have its beginning there as well.

It took us over two years to develop and plan this first meeting—adult learners working together at their best. I wrote the program, although at times I was not sure where I was going or what I was doing. Still, I knew it was going to happen. In a way I couldn't screw it up: It was going to happen with or without me because it was *meant* to happen.

One of the biggest surprises was how many people we had to turn away from the meeting because we only had accommodations for 48 people. I received phone calls from many professionals in the literacy field whom I had to turn away. One person even said, "I'll sweep the floors, cook or whatever it takes just so I can be there to witness this."

I had to say, "I'm sorry, but we don't even have standing room."

## At the Highlander

Our first meeting took place the last weekend of April, 1998. As I left for Tennessee I couldn't help but think of my early school days and wonder what my teachers would think of me having created this movement. Would they even believe I was capable of such a thing?

Most of us arrived on Thursday afternoon. I gave a short speech, a pep talk to get us started. The Highlander provided music for that evening but I, the other five Board members and the moderators had our heads together to go over our plans for the following morning. Some of the attendees, who were coming from all over the country, had not arrived so our official start would be on Friday.

In the morning it was time to begin this long-anticipated event. I walked into the "fireplace room" with its comfortable rocking chairs, where the meetings would be held. We started with some introductions and welcome speeches, then began the process of determining what we needed to do to make this organization come together. Just getting everyone on the same page took some doing. We all came from different perspectives and different levels of maturity with literacy. People had a tendency to get sidetracked, which delayed the progress we would like to have made, but we finished enough to get us up and running.

Two of the members, Jane Hugo from Laubach and Jon Randall from Literacy Volunteers of America, took turns acting as moderators to help us develop our mission statement and bylaws. Besides creating a national organization the primary goal of this undertaking was to develop leaders among the New Readers and generate public awareness of our challenges. This would include lobbying, maintaining tutoring programs and creating more awareness within the educational world of the needs of New Readers. We elected officers and increased our board from five members to ten. Long after departing on Sunday

I was so excited about what we had accomplished that I was in a cloud. I could not believe we'd pulled it off.

## Going National

A year later, in 1999, VALUE held its first national conference in Indianapolis, Indiana. We had held a lot of conference calls to prepare for this two day event, which took a lot of work, considering that we all had other jobs. Still, it was a very successful first conference, with breakout sessions and speakers. About a hundred new students attended as well. Our board continued to look at the future of VALUE to increase membership and involve more states. We had two kinds of membership: New Readers and Associate Members for organizations and professionals. Only the New Readers had voting privileges.

In January of 2000, six people from VALUE, including me, were invited to attend the National Literacy Summit in Washington D.C. This was sponsored by the Institute. It comprised experts from every phase of adult literacy, there by invitation only, and was well attended by people from all across the nation. It was a valuable opportunity for people and agencies to network and review visions for the future of literacy education. I was invited to speak because I was President of VALUE. The focus of the summit was "How can we go forward with adult literacy?" I talked about what adult learners had accomplished and what VALUE was and how it had been created.

My name was listed in the program as a Literacy Recruiter. Later, when the President of Iowa Central Community College saw this, he decided I should have a more respectable title and named me Literacy Coordinator. I was very proud of this accomplishment because previous coordinators were all educators, not New Readers. I continued to work as Literacy Coordinator for the next 13 years.

## Politics and Courtrooms

Of course Federal programs are always at the mercy of incoming Presidents, and the year George Bush Jr. was elected was no different. He had the opportunity to replace everyone on the advisory board, and did so. He also changed the focus of the program from adult literacy to childhood literacy.

I was at home in Eagle Grove when I received an anonymous phone call inviting me to go to the next board meeting for the National Institute for Literacy. The caller told me they would pay my way to attend because they wanted me to talk to the board about how my life had changed by becoming a Fellow. I wanted to do what I could to save the National Institute and to not lose adult literacy from the agenda, so I looked for a way to do whatever I could.

I had previously met Carmella Border, the owner of Border's Books, who was the chair of the newly formed advisory council to the National Institute for Literacy. Since I had a connection with her I decided to email her and ask if I could speak at their next meeting. My goal was to make the Board aware of what NIFL had done for New Readers like me and to not abandon this program. She wrote back giving me permission to speak at their quarterly meeting in Washington, D.C.

I actually gave one of my better talks and closed by saying, "I want you to know that adult learners have many scars from their challenges that make it difficult for them to make changes. Adult learners need to accept their challenges and find a way to make accommodations. Without the nation supporting them I am afraid many will lose their way and what they have accomplished because of the Institute."

After I finished my speech, I walked around and shook hands and gave people handouts I had written for the internet about adult literacy. I could tell that about half were interested and the other half didn't really care what I had to say. In the end, the National Institute for Literacy was eliminated and parts of it were absorbed into the Department of Education, which has since become wrapped up in *No Child Left Behind*.

I felt empty and disappointed that an agency that had had such an important role in literacy was gone. Adult learners had lost the only national voice they'd ever had. I felt like we'd reached a dead end. I hoped that Pro Literacy would be able to pick up the slack and give adult learners the voice they needed to keep fighting.

It was around this time that I received a traffic ticket for not wearing a seatbelt. Since I had never been in a courtroom before I decided to go to the court date. There were about 70 people present so I headed for one of the few seats left in the front of the room. There was a piece of paper on the chair and I asked the lady next to me if someone was sitting there. She said no, so I placed the paper on the table ahead of me and took a seat.

The judge entered and began hearing cases, starting with the person two seats to my left. But before he heard each case he would first ask the citizen if he or she had read the paper on our chairs. When he came I said "No, because I can't read very well," and I asked him to read it to me.

The room went so quiet you could have heard a pin drop.

"No," the judge said, "I won't read it to you. But I will tell you what it says."

I guess I helped him understand that not everyone can read, and let the other people in the room know that some people have hidden disabilities. We are not all alike.

## Chapter 19

# Illiteracy's Daily Impact

## Living Room Language

My connections and relationships in the world of literacy kept taking me in new and different directions. I always tried to stay vigilant to those opportunities and connections, and soon began to learn about a new kind of literacy, at least new to me . . . health literacy. My definition of health literacy is "helping medical practitioners develop an awareness of the need to improve communication with the lay person so the shame of not understanding is removed." The goal of health literacy is to encourage medical practitioners to speak in "living room language" so that their patients—including those with learning disabilities—can fully understand their health situations.

Dr. David Rosen, whom I initially met when I was a Fellow for the National Institute for Literacy, gave my name to a woman who had a grant from the pharmaceutical company Pfizer to involve New Readers in health literacy. She invited six other New Readers and me, all from the United States, along with seven New Readers from Canada, to write about some of our medical experiences; she would submit these reports to the conference. As it happened I had just completed three medical appointments at three different sites so I had fresh experiences to talk about—and of course Wanda helped me write about the visits. I was invited to attend the Second Canadian Conference on Literacy and Health in Ottawa,, Canada, on scholarship from Pfizer, all expenses paid.

I decided to post the medical experiences that Wanda and I had written about on ListServ, and a doctor from Harvard and another from Emory emailed me with supportive statements. They actually praised me for writing and encouraged me to do more of it. Someone from the American Medical Association saw this same Listserv report and contacted me to join in on a conference call to answer questions about my experiences.

The above events were scheduled, but I first had to travel to New York to have an organizational meeting with the VALUE board and to lobby for funding.

All the members of the VALUE committee visited several tutoring programs in the city, to show our support. The tour leader asked our group if someone wanted to talk and because I was President I spoke up and told the students, who were predominately black, what a good job they were doing and to keep on going. Calvin Miles, who was a member of our group and also African American, looked at me afterward and said, "They've probably never heard a white person say any of those words to them before."

The next day, as we were going down in an elevator following a visit to another program, I felt pains in my chest. When we got outside on the sidewalk I had to sit down on the ground. I told the others I needed help. They were all so stunned they didn't know what to do. A rabbi came out of nowhere, or so it seemed, stuck an aspirin under my tongue and put oxygen on me while someone else called an ambulance. The hospital was across the street so the EMT staff gave me a nitroglycerin tablet and carried me over on a gurney.

I was 69 years old and had been working on literacy issues for fourteen years, and I didn't want my work to be done. When they got me across the street a little lady in a white uniform came alongside me.

"Where's the doctor?" I asked.

"I am the doctor," she replied. Everyone was running in every direction just like in the movies. The doctor hooked me up to an IV, someone else drew blood and they told me I was having a heart attack right then, at that moment. They added medicine called a "clot buster" to the IV and told me it might hurt a bit. They weren't exaggerating. Each time my heart pumped I felt like someone was hitting me in the chest—three times in all before the doctor told me the blood clot had broken loose and I was going to be okay.

After they observed me for about a half-hour they took me to a room where the head doctor decided to do an angiogram. I told her I had a conference in Canada and she said "You might be able to make it." From the angiogram they learned that I had three blocked arteries. Sure enough, I had to cancel both my trip to Canada and the AMA conference call.

Meanwhile the police called Wanda in Iowa to tell her I'd had a heart attack. After phone calls to various family members Kelli told Wanda she'd take care of getting airline tickets. Kelli and Wanda's flights connected in Cincinnati, from which they flew to New York City together.

My surgery was performed two days later. I was in the hospital for about a week and then in a rehab center for a couple of weeks. The medical people told me I was doing well, probably because of me being a runner. Prior to the heart attack I'd been running about three days a week, training for the 5K's that I loved participating in. They finally released me to return to Iowa but the trip was physically challenging and I needed another month to recoup enough strength to return to my regular activities.

On the advice of my doctors, during the next conference call of the VALUE committee I resigned as President. Wanda and Kelli also wanted me to resign, and since I knew that running a national organization meant enduring a lot of pressure, I agreed. I was still President Emeritus and VALUE was still being run to develop leadership, but I moved on to focus on Iowa and helping New Readers develop community skills.

About three weeks later I contacted the American Medical Association and explained why I hadn't been able to participate in the conference call. They invited me to help in the production of a video to be entitled *Help Your Patient Understand*, which would be given to medical practitioners to help them comprehend the literacy needs of their patients.

The production ended up being put on hold for about two years because the AMA needed to get money together to produce the video, so meanwhile I focused on the Iowa New Readers. I was also still a Literacy Recruiter for the community college, and serving on the board of the Student Coalition for Action in Literacy Education (SCALES). In that capacity I travelled to North Carolina several times a year for meetings and also attended the national conference. All this came about after I founded VALUE.

# How Does Literacy Affect Voting?

The New Readers of Iowa selected "voting literacy" as their new project to tackle. As a nation we had just completed the 2000 elections and the voting fiasco in Florida pointed the way. As a member of the Democratic Party I was invited to hear a speech being given by Secretary of State (Iowa) Chet Culver. I hoped to use this opportunity to make contact with him so I could set something up to improve the voting in Iowa.

Since Kelli had worked in political circles I called her and said, "Kelli, I need some advice. Since I'm going to be at a speech where Secretary of State Culver is speaking, what would be a good way to talk with him?"

"Dad," Kelli said, "I suggest you watch as Culver comes in the door. He'll probably have two aides with him; see which one you think is more approachable. As soon as you get the aide's attention, make your move."

During Culver's speech I used Kelli's advice to buttonhole one of the aides. I explained about the New Readers of Iowa and how we would like to make sure the ballots in Iowa were user friendly for adult learners and not liable to create a problem like the one Florida had experienced. The aide took my name and address and thanked me for the information.

About a month later I received a letter from Secretary of State Culver inviting me to attend a meeting about voting. At this meeting three other New Readers and I talked about the problems adult learners deal with when they go to the polls because the ballots are different from one county to the next.

We also invited Secretary Culver to come and talk with the New Readers of Iowa and bring all the different ballots that were used in the State. Mr. Culver was happy to do this. At the meeting we broke off into groups and looked at different ballots from different counties and rated them as good or bad and pointed out things that weren't understood. The South Dakota New Readers group had learned what the Iowa New Readers were doing and asked to participate, so they were present as well. Culver took all the recommendations back to the counties and asked them to consider improving the ballots. He could not actually change the ballots because it was up to each individual county to determine their form, but we created awareness and that was out goal. We also went away from our efforts feeling that we understood voting much better.

## Help Your Patients Understand

When the AMA finally got the funding together to make their video they contacted me about seeking New Readers for the taping. "Well," I said, "I'm going to be speaking at the Illinois State Conference for New Readers this weekend, so why don't you guys come out our way? There will be a lot of New Readers to choose from for interviewing and taping." They thought this was a good idea and agreed to use the conference for their selection and taping.

I contacted the person in charge of the conference and they were not only excited to have the AMA attend, they wanted to put on a reception. I suggested to the AMA people that they wear t-shirts and jeans, not suits, to the reception so as not to intimidate the New Readers. By mingling this way the doctors and their photographers comfortably reached a decision about who to use in the video.

I invited two of the doctors, Mark Williams and Ruth Parker, both from Emory University, to talk with the New Readers about health literacy so there could be an open discussion between the two groups about their needs. I was impressed with how well the doctors handled the questions; my only regret was that the discussion was not taped.

In the end, nine hours of taping produced a twenty minute video. About two years later, the Joint Commission invited Toni Cordell, a New Reader, and myself to be part of a working group to produce a white paper that eventually was entitled "'What Did the Doctor Say?': Improving Health Literacy to Protect Patient Safety." Toni and I felt very comfortable working with this team of professionals. The result was a big step forward in health literacy for people with literacy problems.

## The New Readers Tackle Health Literacy

Everything went so well at the Illinois conference and the AMA, as well as with our work on voting issues that I encouraged The New Readers of Iowa to take on another high profile project for our next conference in 2002. As we discussed possible topics someone mentioned that going to the doctor was always a challenge. We struggled with how to develop a focus. I contacted Audrey Riffenburgh, a health literacy and plain language consultant I had worked with before, and hired her to be the moderator for the conference.

Prior to coming to our conference as the moderator, Audrey met with Dr. Mary Ann Abrams, Health Literacy consultant from the Iowa Health System. Audrey told Dr. Abrams about the request to moderate a conference for the Iowa New Readers and Dr. Abrams asked if she could attend. Audrey called me. "Archie, I'm at another conference and Dr. Mary Ann Abrams from the Iowa Health System wants to know if she can attend your Health Literacy conference." I happily agreed, but never heard from her.

A few weeks later I packed my bags and got in the car to drive to the New Reader Health Conference when I realized I had forgotten something. I ran back inside to pick up my shaving gear from the bathroom and as I opened the door the phone rang. It was Dr. Abrams asking to attend the conference. I was glad I'd gone back into the house that day, it would prove to make all the difference in the future. Dr. Abrams not only attended the conference, she agreed to speak at the end.

After the conference Dr. Abrams invited several New Readers, including myself, to be on a Patient Safety Board. Our role would be to evaluate the needs of patients within different areas of medicine.

In 2003, after a year of being on this Board, Dr. Abrams invited the New Readers of Iowa to put on another health literacy conference with both professionals and New Readers. Dr. Abrams and the Iowa Health System brought in therapists, physicians, nurses and others to meet with New Readers.

We sat down in round tables to discuss and solve struggles and solutions. It was a really good discussion and both sides learned a lot. Drake University brought in some of their pharmacy students to go over medicines with each of the New Readers. The New Readers benefitted from this help, but at the same time the pharmacy students learned valuable skills in working with people who have reading challenges.

Other services offered at the conference included a blood pressure screening and a questionnaire that was read to us regarding depression and mental illness. The medical practitioners benefited as much if not more than the New Readers. We were all beginning to learn what was good medicine for people with reading deficiencies, and New Readers were learning to ask for the things they needed.

The New Readers of Iowa continue to hold yearly conferences with a focus on health literacy, and sometimes include financial and technology literacy as well. Health literacy and general literacy both become stronger when they work together. If the medical professionals know we have literacy problems they can also give us better medical care.

Many questions remain that individuals with reading or learning disabilities need to find answers to from their practitioners. How do adult learners inform practitioners of their needs? Whose responsibility is health literacy? There are those in the medical field who feel that literacy testing should be done before a patient receives medical attention. From their viewpoint that might sound like a good idea, but before making such a decision you need to look through the eyes of the person with literacy problems.

As a dyslexic and an adult learner with reading problems I speak for many other adult learners: We hate having to take yet another written literacy test. People with other kinds of handicaps are not continually asked to expose their weaknesses. While there is no physical pain in taking a written test, the mental challenge produces a lot of frustration inside us. We grew up feeling humiliated because of our poor literacy skills, and written tests are seen as a step backward for us. It turns us away.

Health literacy as an issue has been around for some time. The New Readers of Iowa are not starting a health literacy movement but rather are showing the health field a real face by attending health meetings and conferences and contributing our experiences.

In 2003, after I retired from my recruiter job, I was invited to speak at a conference that the Iowa Health System was putting on for medical office staff to gain an understanding of people like me. There were about sixty people in the audience, including a man from my past who lived nearby; I'd invited him because I thought he might appreciate being there. He had influenced my life as a kid: Bill Nelson, the National winning wrestler who taught me how to be a better football player and opened all kinds of doors for me.

As I shared my story with the audience about growing up dyslexic, Bill had tears coming down his face. After the program several people, including Bill and his wife, came up to talk with me. Bill couldn't believe how I'd gotten up there and talked without notes. Even I thought it was one of my better speeches. It was just another reminder to me of how successful my words were when I didn't use notes, just my good memory and the third dimension of my brain. I will never be healed from my dyslexia, so I just have to use my strengths to do the best that I can.

## Losing the Love of My Life

In the spring of 2006 my wife Wanda was diagnosed with a very aggressive form of cancer. Six weeks later she was gone. We'd had over 40 years of happiness together. She'd been there for me through all my literacy struggles. She'd been my right hand and a part of who I eventually became.

After her death I initially wanted to give up hope, but I knew she would want me to keep going. I gradually began to get reinvolved in my passion for literacy. I returned to it in pieces, but quite honestly I've never quite gotten back to where I was before Wanda passed away. Even writing these words has made me sad, and I have shed some tears.

But there have been personal gains as well. I am very proud of Kelli, who married and along with her husband produced two children. I guess that means I am a grandpa. Kelli is now a social worker with the Wisconsin prison system. Just like her mother, Kelli inspired my growth with regard to my learning challenges and has been an important ally all along. Through all these years I think Kelli has taught me more than I ever taught her.

## Financial Aid Training for New Readers

In 2009, while I was serving on the Board of the Iowa Literacy Council, I decided to approach another board member, who also worked for Wells Fargo, about sponsoring an Iowa New Reader Conference on Financial Literacy.

She thought it was a good idea, so we met with other Wells Fargo officials and the decision was made to go ahead. Wells Fargo felt that everyone would benefit, including them because of the good public relations it would create for their company.

Basically, the conference was focused on money management, such as not buying things you don't really need, managing debt, how to use credit cards, and using your tax refund to pay off debt rather than just spending it. I felt that this really helped the New Readers be more conscious of how to handle their money.

## National Award 2010

In 2010, the National Institute for Literacy formed a coalition and gave awards recognizing people for leadership in literacy.

I received a call from the president of the National Institute informing me that I had been selected to receive one of five awards, and the details of travel. I was surprised and wondered why I was getting the award when there were so many people like me who could be recognized. I called Kelli and other friends to tell them about it. Later my local newspaper interviewed me and wrote an article about some of the things I had accomplished. It was a really great event because I got to see a lot of people I haven't seen for a long time. I felt proud that they thought of me, and I have the plaque hanging in my house.

# What I Believe

*Historically literacy has been brought to the forefront as our country focused on the rights of people. Black rights, women and voting and now learning disabled.*
—*Forest Cheeseman, author*

## Join the Mainstream

When I surrendered my secret inability to read to the help of my wife and daughter, sought a way to be tested and finally committed to tutoring, I opened myself to my disability and helped myself grow. I found people who saw something in me and gave me encouragement.

I want this book to help New Readers learn to believe in themselves so they can advocate for what they need. That's why I formed VALUE and continue to work to advance all forms of literacy. Please use my examples of chance encounters and not missing opportunities to help you find your way, as I did. We also need parents and professionals to take on leadership roles in all areas of literacy as well as advocating for those who can't.

I have worked with many leaders and held many different leadership roles. Therefore I believe I am qualified to define a good leader: *A leader is someone who knows how to develop relationships with other people, knows his or her environment, understands the strengths and weaknesses of the people they are working with, knows how to develop connections outside their organization to broaden their strength, and most importantly accepts that the buck stops with them.*

I encourage others who struggle to read to join the mainstream of life. By doing this your life will improve. Think of all your connections and the people in your life as being inside a circle. Now imagine expanding that circle by finding more people like yourself with reading challenges, and opening yourself to new opportunities. Your circle will widen, just as mine did when I stopped pushing people away. I found out I wasn't alone when I let society know I was there.

Until recently people with reading problems haven't really had a voice. I've tried to represent that voice by advocating for adult literacy. I don't do this for just myself. I do it so everyone who struggles with reading can have a chance to live their lives more fully. I want those of you who are reading challenged to not ask for more than what you deserve, but not settle for less than what you should have.

I have been involved in literacy since 1985 and have come full circle. I can see the parts of literacy that span educational, medical and community issues. I challenge all of you reading this to make it your mission to bring the parts together. The first step is to make the needs of New Readers known, and the second is to encourage learning disabled children and adult learners to believe in themselves and step up and look for answers. I would like to see more adult learners involved, too; this will increase the voice for literacy.

It seems that sometimes experts aren't aware of how important it is to hear from those of us who are reading-challenged. There are people who don't know how to respect the lack of credentials of many New Readers, and therefore overlook their value or knowledge. Bureaucracy can get in the way, as well as the egos of individuals and their credentials. I challenge those of you in these professions to not lose the human quality of looking at individuals and respecting those who are learning-disabled and the difficulties they face. Take the time to listen to them.

New Readers, dyslexics and parents of learning disabled children need to challenge the educational system and the political leaders to keep humanity and respect present in their work. We don't want to tell people how to think, we want to teach them to think for themselves. Initially I told myself *I can't do this*. Then I found out I could, in my own way.

So, in spite of all the challenges I faced from childhood, I eventually embraced my learning challenges and used them to improve the world of literacy, one step at a time. My hope is that by sharing my story I can help you learn ways to help yourself or others who have challenges to face. Learning that I was dyslexic, facing my problems and talking about them made me feel free for the first time in my life. I hope you will find inspiration in my story.

If I were walking down a beach and found a bottle and opened it and a genie came out and granted me one wish, I would never wish that I was not dyslexic. Dyslexics think and process in three dimensions while most people process in two. I would never want to lose that third dimension. Instead I would use my wish to go back in time long enough to find the little boy who sat in the back of the room staring out the window, put my arm around him and squeeze a smile onto his face.

Thanks for reading my book.

# Resources

## Publications

Willard, Archie. "Staying in a Literacy Program," published in 1998 by the National Center for the Study of Adult Learning and Literacy.

"The Annual Review of Adult Learning and Literacy," published in 2000 by the National Center for the Study of Adult Learning and Literacy.

"Making the Case, Adult Education and Literacy: Key to America's Future," published in 2002 by the Council for the Advancement of Adult Literacy.

"What Did the Doctor Say?" Improving Health Literacy to Protect Patient Safety, 2007 by the Joint Commission.

"Plain Language Pediatric Patient Education," Copyright 2008 by the American Academy of Pediatrics.

Cooper, Jay. "New Reader Has Advice for Public Health Workers and Partners," Copyright 2009, for *Plain and Simple,* a health literacy project for Iowa.

## Videos

*Help Your Patients Understand,* Copyright 2008 by the American Medical Association Foundation and American Medical Association.

*Health Literacy Out Loud,* HLOL Podcast #3: "Archie Willard Talks About Struggling to Read."

## YouTube Videos

"Growing up Dyslexic," 2008 Iowa Literacy Resource Center

"Learning to Read," 2008 Iowa Literacy Resource Center

"New Readers of Iowa," 2008 University of Iowa / Department of Education

## Boards

*Iowa Literacy Council*, Iowa State Department of Education, 1994-present.

SCALE (Student Coalition for Action in Literacy Education) University of North Carolina, Chapel Hill, 1999-2005

*Society of Hospital Medicine*, Emory University Medical School, 2005-present

*Reach Out and Read*, Iowa branch, 2006-present

# About the Authors

 Archie Willard learned to read at the age of 54. Being diagnosed as dyslexic was the breakthrough that helped him embark on the path to acquiring the skills he needed to learn to read.

Sharing what he'd learned along the way, and wanting to improve conditions for other who couldn't read, led him to become an advocate for literacy. Mr. Willard is a Fellow with the National Institute for Literacy, and travels throughout the U.S. and abroad to learn about and consult with others about their literacy programs. Archie is the founder of VALUE (Voice of Adult Literacy United for Education), which he created to promote leadership in adults with literacy problems. Mr. Willard divides his time between Iowa and Arizona. The author can be contacted at www.thelastreaderstanding.com.

 Colleen O'Reilly Wiemerslage is a former teacher, counselor and writer. She has taught every grade level including college level, and writes a newspaper parenting column online. Colleen and her husband divide their time between Wisconsin and Arizona. Colleen can be contacted at: www.thelastreaderstanding.com

# Other Books by
# Bettie Youngs Book Publishers

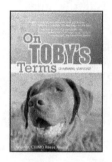

## On Toby's Terms
### Charmaine Hammond

*On Toby's Terms* is an endearing story of a beguiling creature who teaches his owners that, despite their trying to teach him how to be the dog they want, he is the one to lay out the terms of being the dog he needs to be. This insight would change their lives forever.

Simply a beautiful book about life, love, and purpose. —Jack Canfield, compiler, *Chicken Soup for the Soul* series

In a perfect world, every dog would have a home and every home would have a dog like Toby! —Nina Siemaszko, actress, *The West Wing*

This is a captivating, heartwarming story and we are very excited about bringing it to film. —Steve Hudis, Producer

### Soon to be a major motion picture!

ISBN: 978-0-9843081-4-9 • $15.95

## Diary of a Beverly Hills Matchmaker
### Marla Martenson

Marla takes her readers for a hilarious romp through her days in an exclusive matchmaking agency. From juggling the demands of out-of-touch clients and trying to meet the capricious demands of an insensitive boss to the ups and downs of her own marriage with a husband who doesn't think that she is "domestic" enough, Marla writes with charm and self-effacement about the universal struggles of finding the love of our lives—and knowing it.

Martenson's irresistible quick wit will have you rolling on the floor. —Megan Castran, international YouTube Queen

ISBN: 978-0-9843081-0-1 • $14.95

# The Maybelline Story—And the Spirited Family Dynasty Behind It

## Sharrie Williams

Throughout the twentieth century, Maybelline inflated, collapsed, endured, and thrived in tandem with the nation's upheavals. Williams, to avoid unwanted scrutiny of his private life, cloistered himself behind the gates of his Rudolph Valentino Villa and ran his empire from a distance. This never before told story celebrates the life of a man whose vision rocketed him to success along with the woman held in his orbit: his brother's wife, Evelyn Boecher—who became his lifelong fascination and muse. A fascinating and inspiring story, a tale both epic and intimate, alive with the clash, the hustle, the music, and dance of American enterprise.

A richly told story of a forty-year, white-hot love triangle that fans the flames of a major worldwide conglomerate. —**Neil Shulman, Associate Producer,** *Doc Hollywood*

Salacious! Engrossing! There are certain stories, so dramatic, so sordid, that they seem positively destined for film; this is one of them. —*New York Post*

ISBN: 978-0-9843081-1-8 • $18.95

# It Started with Dracula
## The Count, My Mother, and Me

## Jane Congdon

The terrifying legend of Count Dracula silently skulking through the Transylvania night may have terrified generations of filmgoers, but the tall, elegant vampire captivated and electrified a young Jane Congdon, igniting a dream to one day see his mysterious land of ancient castles and misty hollows. Four decades later she finally takes her long-awaited trip—never dreaming that it would unearth decades-buried memories, and trigger a life-changing inner journey. A memoir full of surprises, Jane's story is one of hope, love—and second chances.

Unfinished business can surface when we least expect it. *It Started with Dracula* is the inspiring story of two parallel journeys: one a carefully planned vacation and the other an astonishing and unexpected detour in healing a wounded heart. —**Charles Whitfield, MD, bestselling author of** *Healing the Child Within*

An elegantly written and cleverly told story. An electrifying read. —**Diane Bruno, CISION Media**

ISBN: 978-1-936332-10-6 • $15.95

# The Rebirth of Suzzan Blac

## Suzzan Blac

A horrific upbringing and then abduction into the sex slave industry would all but kill Suzzan's spirit to live. But a happy marriage and two children brought love—and forty-two stunning paintings, art so raw that it initially frightened even the artist. "I hid the pieces for 15 years," says Suzzan, "but just as with the secrets in this book, I am slowing sneaking them out, one by one by one." Now a renowned artist, her work is exhibited world-wide.

A story of inspiration, truth and victory.

A solid memoir about a life reconstructed. Chilling, thrilling, and thought provoking. —Pearry Teo, Producer, *The Gene Generation*

ISBN: 978-1-936332-22-9 • $16.95

# Blackbird Singing in the Dead of Night

## What to Do When God Won't Answer

### Updated Edition with Study Guide

## Gregory L. Hunt

Pastor Greg Hunt had devoted nearly thirty years to congregational ministry, helping people experience God and find their way in life. Then came his own crisis of faith and calling. While turning to God for guidance, he finds nothing. Neither his education nor his religious involvements could prepare him for the disorienting impact of the experience.

Alarmed, he tries an experiment. The result is startling—and changes his life entirely.

In this most beautiful memoir, Greg Hunt invites us into an unsettling time in his life, exposes the fault lines of his faith, and describes the path he walked into and out of the dark. Thanks to the trail markers he leaves along the way, he makes it easier for us to find our way, too. —Susan M. Heim, co-author, *Chicken Soup for the Soul, Devotional Stories for Women*

Compelling. If you have ever longed to hear God whispering a love song into your life, read this book. —Gary Chapman, *NY Times* bestselling author, *The Love Languages of God*

ISBN: 978-0-9882848-9-0 • $18.95

# DON CARINA
## WWII Mafia Heroine

### *Ron Russell*

A father's death in Southern Italy in the 1930s—a place where women who can read are considered unfit for marriage—thrusts seventeen-year-old Carina into servitude as a "black widow," a legal head of the household who cares for her twelve siblings. A scandal forces her into a marriage to Russo, the "Prince of Naples."

By cunning force, Carina seizes control of Russo's organization and disguising herself as a man, controls the most powerful of Mafia groups for nearly a decade. Discovery is inevitable: Interpol has been watching. Nevertheless, Carina survives to tell her children her stunning story of strength and survival.

ISBN: 978-0-9843081-9-4 • $15.95

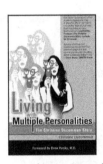

# *Living with Multiple Personalities*
## The Christine Ducommun Story

### *Christine Ducommun*

Christine Ducommun was a happily married wife and mother of two, when—after moving back into her childhood home—she began to experience panic attacks and a series of bizarre flashbacks. Eventually diagnosed with Dissociative Identity Disorder (DID), Christine's story details an extraordinary twelve-year ordeal unraveling the buried trauma of her past and the daunting path she must take to heal from it. Therapy helps to identify Christine's personalities and understand how each helped her cope with her childhood, but she'll need to understand their influence on her adult life.

Fully reawakened and present, the personalities compete for control of Christine's mind as she bravely struggles to maintain a stable home for her growing children. In the shadows, her life tailspins into unimaginable chaos—bouts of drinking and drug abuse, sexual escapades, theft and fraud—leaving her to believe she may very well be losing the battle for her sanity. Nearing the point of surrender, a breakthrough brings integration.

A brave story of identity, hope, healing and love.

Reminiscent of the Academy Award-winning *A Beautiful Mind*, this true story will have you on the edge of your seat. Spellbinding! —Josh Miller, Producer

ISBN: 978-0-9843081-5-6 • $16.95

# Amazing Adventures of a Nobody

## Leon Logothetis

Tired of his disconnected life and uninspiring job, Leon leaves it all behind—job, money, home even his cell phone—and hits the road with nothing but the clothes on his back. His journey from Times Square to the Hollywood sign relying on the kindness of strangers and the serendipity of the open road, inspires a dramatic and life changing transformation.

A gem of a book; endearing, engaging and inspiring. —Catharine Hamm, *Los Angeles Times* Travel Editor

Leon reaches out to every one of us who has ever thought about abandoning our routines and living a life of risk and adventure. His tales of learning to rely on other people are warm, funny, and entertaining. If you're looking to find meaning in this disconnected world of ours, this book contains many clues. —*Psychology Today*

ISBN: 978-0-9843081-3-2 • $14.95

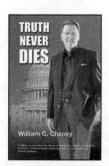

# Truth Never Dies

## William C. Chasey

A lobbyist for some 40 years, William C. Chasey represented some of the world's most prestigious business clients and twenty-three foreign governments before the US Congress. His integrity never questioned.

All that changed when Chasey was hired to forge communications between Libya and the US Congress. A trip he took with a US Congressman for discussions with then Libyan leader Muammar Qadhafi forever changed Chasey's life. Upon his return, his bank accounts were frozen, clients and friends had been advised not to take his calls.

Things got worse: the CIA, FBI, IRS, and the Federal Judiciary attempted to coerce him into using his unique Libyan access to participate in a CIA-sponsored assassination plot of the two Libyans indicted for the bombing of Pan Am flight 103. Chasey's refusal to cooperate resulted in the destruction of his reputation, a six-year FBI investigation and sting operation, financial ruin, criminal charges, and incarceration in federal prison.

A somber tale, a thrilling read. —Gary Chafetz, author, *The Perfect Villain: John McCain and the Demonization of Lobbyist Jack Abramoff*

ISBN: 978-1-936332-46-5 • $24.95

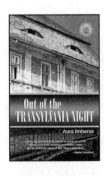

# Out of the Transylvania Night

## Aura Imbarus

### A Pulitzer-Prize entry

"I'd grown up in the land of Transylvania, homeland to Dracula, Vlad the Impaler, and worse, dictator Nicolae Ceausescu," writes the author. "Under his rule, like vampires, we came to life after sundown, hiding our heirloom jewels and documents deep in the earth." Fleeing to the US to rebuild her life, she discovers a startling truth about straddling two cultures and striking a balance between one's dreams and the sacrifices that allow a sense of "home."

Aura's courage shows the degree to which we are all willing to live lives centered on freedom, hope, and an authentic sense of self. Truly a love story! —Nadia Comaneci, Olympic Champion

A stunning account of erasing a past, but not an identity. —Todd Greenfield, 20th Century Fox

ISBN: 978-0-9843081-2-5 • $14.95

# Universal Co-opetition
## Nature's Fusion of Co-operation and Competition

## V Frank Asaro

A key ingredient in business success is competition—and cooperation. Too much of one or the other can erode personal and organizational goals. This book identifies and explains the natural, fundamental law that unifies the apparently opposing forces of cooperation and competition. By finding this synthesis point in a variety of situations—from the personal to the organizational—this is the ultimate recipe for individual or group success.

"Your extraordinary book has given me valuable insights." —Spencer Johnson, author, *Who Moved My Cheese*

ISBN: 978-1-936332-08-3 • $15.95

# The Morphine Dream

### Don Brown with Boston Globe Pulitzer nominated Gary S. Chafetz

At 36, high-school dropout and a failed semi-profes-
sional ballplayer Donald Brown hit bottom when an industrial accident left him immobilized. But Brown had a dream
while on a morphine drip after surgery: he imagined him-
self graduating from Harvard Law School (he was a classmate of Barack Omaba)
and walking across America. Brown realizes both seemingly unreachable goals, and
achieves national recognition as a legal crusader for minority homeowners. This
intriguing tale of his long walk—both physical and metaphorical—is an amazing
story of loss, gain and the power of perseverance.

"An incredibly inspirational memoir." —Alan M. Dershowitz, professor,
Harvard Law School

ISBN: 978-1-936332-25-0 • $24.95

# Hostage of Paradox: A Memoir

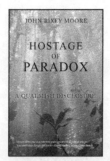

### John Rixey Moore

A profound odyssey of a college graduate who enlists
in the military to avoid being drafted, becomes a Green
Beret Airborne Ranger, and is sent to Vietnam where he is
plunged into high-risk, deep-penetration operations under
contract to the CIA—work for which he was neither specifi-
cally trained nor psychologically prepared, yet for which he
is ultimately highly decorated. Moore survives, but can't shake the feeling that some
in the military didn't care if he did, or not. Ultimately he would have a 40-year
career in television and film.

A compelling story told with extraordinary insight, disconcerting reality, and
engaging humor. —David Hadley, actor, *China Beach*

ISBN: 978-1-936332-37-3 • $29.95

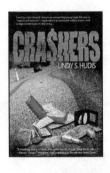

# Crashers
## *A Tale of "Cappers" and "Hammers"*

### Lindy S. Hudis

The illegal business of fraudulent car accidents is a multi-million dollar racket, involving unscrupulous medical providers, personal injury attorneys, and the cooperating passengers involved in the accidents. Innocent people are often swept into it.

Newly engaged Nathan and Shari, who are swimming in mounting debt, were easy prey: seduced by an offer from a stranger to move from hard times to good times in no time, Shari finds herself the "victim" in a staged auto accident. Shari gets her payday, but breaking free of this dark underworld will take nothing short of a miracle.

A riveting story of love, life—and limits. A non-stop thrill ride. —Dennis "Danger" Madalone, stunt coordinator for the television series, *Castle*

ISBN: 978-1-936332-27-4 • $16.95

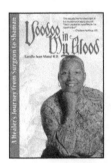

# *Voodoo in My Blood*
## *A Healer's Journey from Surgeon to Shaman*

### Carolle Jean-Murat, M.D.

Born and raised in Haiti to a family of healers, US trained physician Carolle Jean-Murat came to be regarded as a world-class surgeon. But her success harbored a secret: in the operating room, she could quickly intuit the root cause of her patient's illness, often times knowing she could help the patient without having to put her under the knife. Carolle knew that to fellow surgeons, her intuition was best left unmentioned. But when the devastating earthquake hit Haiti and Carolle returned to help—she had to acknowledge the shaman she had become.

This mesmerizing story takes us inside the secret world of voodoo as a healing practice, and sheds light on why it remains a mystery to most and shunned by many.

"A beautiful memoir." —Christiane Northrup, M.D.

"A masterpiece! Truly enlightening. A personal story you won't soon forget." —Adrianne Belafonte-Bizemeyer

ISBN: 978-1-936332-05-2 • $24.95

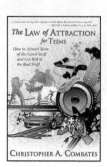

# The Law of Attraction for Teens
## How to Get More of the Good Stuff, and Get Rid of the Bad Stuff!

### Christopher Combates

Whether it's getting better grades, creating better relationships with your friends, parents, or teachers, or getting a date for the prom, the Law of Attraction just might help you bring it about. It works like this: Like attracts like. When we align our goals with our best intentions and highest purpose, when we focus on what we want, we are more likely to bring it about. This book will help teens learn how to think, act, and communicate in the positive way.

ISBN: 978-1-936332-29-8 • $14.95

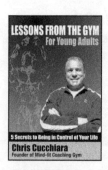

# Lessons from the Gym for Young Adults
## 5 Secrets to Being in Control of Your Life

### Chris Cucchiara

Do you lack self-confidence or have a difficult time making decisions? Do you ever have a tough time feeling a sense of purpose and belonging? Do you worry that you don't measure up? Or that you're doing what other people want of you, instead of what you want?

Growing up, Chris Cucchiara felt the same, until he joined a gym. The lessons he learned helped him gain the confidence he needed to set and achieve goals. In *Lessons from the Gym for Yourg Adults,* Chris shares his experiences and powerful insights and shows you how to:

- develop mental toughness (a life without fear, stress, and anger);
- develop an attitude to get and stay healthy and fit;
- build an "athlete for life" mentality that stresses leadership and excellence as a mindset; and,
- stay motivated, and set and achieve goals that matter.

ISBN: 978-1-936332-38-0 • $14.95

# The Tortoise Shell Code

## V Frank Asaro

Off the coast of Southern California, the Sea Diva, a tuna boat, sinks. Members of the crew are missing and what happened remains a mystery. Anthony Darren, a renowned and wealthy lawyer at the top of his game, knows the boat's owner and soon becomes involved in the case. As the case goes to trial, a missing crew member is believed to be at fault, but new evidence comes to light and the finger of guilt points in a completely unanticipated direction.

Now Anthony must pull together all his resources to find the truth in what has happened and free a wrongly accused man—as well as untangle himself. Fighting despair, he finds that the recent events have called much larger issues into question. As he struggles to right this terrible wrong, Anthony makes new and enlightening discoveries in his own life-long battle for personal and global justice.

"One of the most interesting and exciting books I've read. This will have you on the edge of your seat." —Ron Russell, author of *Don Carina*

ISBN: 978-1-936332-60-1 • $24.95

# The Girl Who Gave Her Wish Away

## Sharon Babineau

### Foreword by Graig Kielburger,
### Co-Founder, FREE THE CHILDREN

The Children's Wish Foundation approached lovely fourteen-year-old Maddison Babineau just after she received her cancer diagnosis. "You can have anything," they told her, "a Disney cruise? The chance to meet your favorite movie star? A five thousand dollar shopping spree?"

Maddie knew exactly what she wanted. She had recently been moved to tears after watching a television program about the plight of orphaned children in an African village. Maddie's wish? To ease the suffering of these children half-way across the world. Despite the ravishing cancer, she became an indefatigable fund-raiser for "her children."

In *The Girl Who Gave Wish Away*, her mother reveals Maddie's remarkable journey of providing hope and future to the village children who had filled her heart.

A special story, heartwarming and reassuring.

ISBN: 978-1-936332-96-0 • $18.95

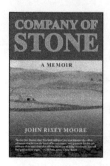

# Company of Stone
## John Rixey Moore

While on a lone tour in the rugged Scottish highlands, John Moore flees a freezing rainstorm by seeking shelter in a remote monastery. He nestles into the brotherhood—hardly believing what he learns about blind chance and the best of human nature. Later, a chance conversation overheard in a village pub steers him to become a rock drill operator in a large industrial gold mine. The dangers he encounters among the provocative, frightening, lost men of the mine, who seek anonymity in a world deep underground, challenge both his endurance and his sense of self.

With sensitivity and humor, Moore explores the unexpected lessons learned in the strange but rich monasticism of forgotten men—a brotherhood housed in crumbling medieval masonry and, one shared in the dangerous rocky depths of the gold mine.

An engaging adventure of discovery.

ISBN: 978-1-936332-44-1 • $19.95

# Mr. Joe
## Tales from a Haunted Life
## Joseph Barnett and Jane Congdon

"Thrilling, thoughtful, elegantly told. So much more than a ghost story." —Cyrus Webb, CEO, Conversation Book Club

Do you believe in ghosts? Nor did Joseph Barnett until the winter he was fired from his career job and became a school custodian to make ends meet. The fact that the eighty-five-year-old school where he now worked was built near a cemetery had barely registered with Joe when he was assigned the graveyard shift. But soon, walking the dim halls alone at night, listening to the wind howl outside, Joe was confronted with a series of bizarre and terrifying occurrences.

It wasn't just the ghosts of the graveyard shift that haunted him. Once the child of a distant father and an alcoholic mother, now a man devastated by a failed marriage, fearful of succeeding as a single dad, and challenged by an overwhelming illness, Joe is haunted by his own personal ghosts.

The story of Joseph's challenges and triumphs emerges as an eloquent metaphor of ghosts, past and present, real and emotional, and how a man puts his beliefs about self—and ghosts—to the test.

"This is truly inspirational work, a very special book—a gift to any reader." —Diane Bruno, CISION Media

ISBN: 978-1-936332-78-6 • $18.95

# Fastest Man in the World

## Tony Volpentest
### Foreword by Ross Perot

Tony Volpentest is a four-time Gold Medalist and five-time World Champion sprinter. He carried the Olympic flame at the 1996 Atlanta Olympics. But it is not so much the medals he sports that make him admirable; it is the grit and determination that got him there. Though born without hands or feet, he is the fastest runner in the world. Tony shares his incredible journey, from the feet that Ross Perot built for him, to his 2012 induction into the Olympic Hall of Fame.

This inspiring story is about the thrill of victory to be sure—winning Olympic Gold—but it is also a reminder about human potential: the ability to push ourselves beyond the ledge of imagination, and to develop grit that fuels indefatigable determination. Simply a powerful story. —**Charlie Huebner, United States Olympic Committee**

ISBN 978-1-936332-00-7 • $16.95

CPSIA information can be obtained
at www.ICGtesting.com
Printed in the USA
LVHW031541140423
744392LV00002B/260